Sep

HORNBY magazine

HORNBY KEY
magazine yearbook

PUBLISHING

Edited by Mike Wild

Whats inside...

20

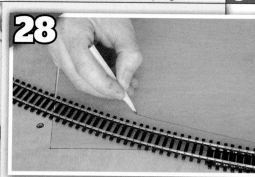

28

We show you how to build solid top and open frame basebaords.

36

Nigel Burkin unveils the secrets of building bogie wagon kits.

42

How to create a model landscape using readily available materials.

EDITORIAL
Editor: Mike Wild
Assistant Editor: Mark Chivers
Contributors: Evan Green-Hughes, Tim Shackleton, NIgel Burkin, Paul Chetter, Julia Scarlett and Ian Wild.
Senior designer: Steve Diggle

REGISTERED OFFICE
Units 1-4, Gwash Way Industrial Estate, Ryhall Road, Stamford, Lincs PE9 1XP

PRINTING
Berforts Information Press
Oxford, Oxfordshire.

ADVERTISING
Advertising: Matt Tipton
Email: matt.tipton@keypublishing.com
Tel: 01780 755131 **Fax:** 01780 757261
Advertising Production: Cheryl Thornburn
Tel: 01780 755131
Fax: 01780 757261
Email: cheryl.thornburn@keypublishing.co.uk

PUBLISHING
Publisher: Adrian Cox
Tel: 01780 755131
Fax: 01780 757261
Email: adrian.cox@keypublishing.com

Executive Chairman: Richard Cox
Managing Director: Adrian Cox
Commercial Director: Ann Saundry
Sales & Marketing Manager: Martin Steele

Key Publishing Ltd,
Units 1-4, Gwash Way Industrial Estate

A Gresley 'J39' 0-6-0
rumbles past Felton
Cement Works with a
pick up goods – next stop
Shortley Bridge.

Welcome

THE SUMMER is always a busy time in the *Hornby Magazine* workshop. Each year we set about building a new project for the Yearbook with a tight three-month timescale from start to finish. This year has been even busier than normal as we've not only been building the layout that fills this book, but also finishing Twelve Trees Junction from *Hornby Magazine Yearbook No 6* for its exhibition debut.

Building a model railway is an enthralling process and one we all thoroughly enjoy, but it never ceases to amaze us just how much work is required in finishing one for an exhibition debut. Fascia panels, lighting rigs, electrics, rolling stock, packing – it all has to be done and in fact this year's project layout, Shortley Bridge and Felton Cement Works, is also set to make its exhibition debut at the Warley National Model Railway Exhibition on the weekend of November 21/22.

Shortley Bridge and Felton Cement Works

is our first foray into building a North Eastern Region themed layout. It is built with 'OO' gauge track and occupies a substantial 12ft x 12ft inclusive of its storage yard. It's a big layout which features a single track branch line, a station and a busy cement works.

The theme for the layout was driven by our desire to take the Operation Build It! terminus station and develop it into a larger project. We had lots of different ideas about how it would happen and you can read all about its gestation and development in this book. We feel the end result is a striking model with a great deal of variety – and we hope you agree.

Variety is what this hobby is all about and we have certainly seen that through the past 12 months. New model releases have continued with some fantastic highlights such as Hatton's LMS Beyer Garratt 2-6-0+0-6-2 as well as an impressive range of new announcements. In fact announcements for new locomotives have

far outstripped the number that have been released, but it keeps the hobby exciting and keeps us wanting more – and perhaps a small windfall to acquire it all at once!

As Summer turned to Autumn we've seen Hornby bounce back in fine style after a period of slow deliveries, and the company seems to be fighting fit again and delivering a constant supply of new products to the marketplace. This is fantastic news for everyone as it brings more reason to be interested in the hobby.

I hope that you enjoy this seventh *Hornby Magazine Yearbook* and that it inspires your own projects big and small.

Happy modelling!

Mike Wild

Mike Wild
Editor, *Hornby Magazine*

Shortley Bridge & Felton Cement Works

MIKE WILD introduces this year's Yearbook project layout and reveals how the Operation Build It! layout from the magazine has become the catalyst for a much larger railway.

MOST OF US SET OUT with a defined scheme for how our projects will be built. We have a size in mind, a location, a scale, theme and purpose. But for this brand new *Hornby Magazine* project we had few of these ideals in place.

We had the scale – it would be 'OO' gauge – and we knew it would be built with code 75 track from the Peco stable. There was no particular location for the layout to be based as it would be built in our workshop for use at exhibitions, so that made its size more flexible. And as for the theme and purpose, our thoughts turned to what we might be able to do with the Operation Build It! terminus

station board which was built as a feature series in HM76-HM83.

This layout featured a single scenic baseboard measuring 6ft x 2ft and on it we had created a small single platform terminus station with a run-round loop and a modest goods yard. Joined to this at one end was a single 4ft x 2ft fiddle yard board which supported five tracks accessed from a fan of points.

In this format it formed an ideal starting point and fitted the bill of the Operation Build It! brief perfectly, but it held potential to become part of something more enthralling – a larger branch line scheme.

Initially we had in mind to keep it as a

terminus and create a 'U' shaped layout from there with a second station with a passing loop on the opposite side of the 'U'. However, even though we had a rough estimate of 12ft x 13ft in mind for the footprint of the whole layout, this scheme didn't offer the operational potential we really wanted.

So it was back to the drawing board and we started thinking again. It had to be a branch line and having covered the Western, Southern and Midland regions in the past three Yearbooks, this time we were aiming for an Eastern/North Eastern Region layout, but with the flexibility of running a smattering of Midland Region motive power alongside the Eastern designs. »

The Operation Build It! terminus station has become the catalyst for Shortley Bridge and Felton Cement Works. The original 6ft x 2ft terminus station board is a great introduction to model railway construction and with in this Yearbook we will be showing you how to take it further.

Diagram 1 - The original plan for this layout was to create a terminus to fiddle yard layout with a through station to one side. While it looked good on paper we wanted more from the finished railway.

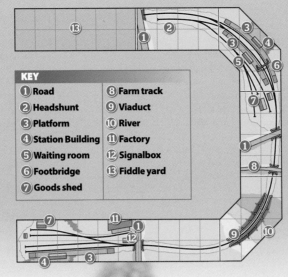

KEY

① Road	⑧ Farm track
② Headshunt	⑨ Viaduct
③ Platform	⑩ River
④ Station Building	⑪ Factory
⑤ Waiting room	⑫ Signalbox
⑥ Footbridge	⑬ Fiddle yard
⑦ Goods shed	

Below: **Cement traffic has become a central theme for Shortley Bridge. A 'WD' 2-8-0 eases a rake of Presflo cement hoppers across Shortley Bridge viaduct heading for Felton Cement Works.**

Giant jigsaw

With a collection of more than 12 layouts built for the magazine since its launch in 2007, we already have a number of components – particularly fiddle yards – that could be reused on new projects. And therein was an idea – the fiddle yards built for Berrybridge and used also for Ashland were still in storage and seemed perfect for use in this new project, particularly during construction.

Now we could start assembling a plan with pre-assembled boards. Sticking with the 12ft x 13ft footprint and the 'U' shape we set the two 4ft x 18in fiddle yard boards at opposite corners then put the Operation Build It! station board in next to one of them. With all this in place – on paper at least for now – we sketched out an idea for the rest of the branch line including turning the Operation

Build It! board into a through station and leading around across open countryside to a second station set on a curve with two platforms and a goods yard. A headshunt long enough to take a locomotive and five wagons was envisaged and it felt like we had the basis of a strong and feasible plan.

Train lengths would be restricted to a locomotive plus three carriages or a locomotive and nine wagons by the length of the turntable fiddle yard boards, but that was plenty for a branch line layout and followed in the tradition established by Berrybridge and Ashland.

While mocking up the layout on paper, shades of Berrybridge returned and memories of one of its traffic flows, cement, came flooding back. It reminded us of how much we'd all enjoyed running that layout which had been built in just 75 hours start to finish

for *Hornby Magazine Yearbook No. 2*. This layout had that same potential, but with a lot more operational flexibility and with the paper plan drawn up we set to work on assembling the baseboards – see feature on pages 14-19 for the full run down on baseboard assembly for this project.

Evolution

With the baseboards assembled the layout continued to evolve. We had set the Operation Build It! baseboard on the right hand side of the 'U' when viewed from the front, but when it came to mocking up the track arrangement on the new baseboards it became clear very quickly that this wouldn't work.

Happily at this stage of construction the boards were only being held together with G-clamps meaning that the final design could

continue evolving as we moved on with the project. So after about 10 minutes in our original planned position, the Operation Build It! station was un-clamped from the corner board and swapped to the opposite side. This gave a much better curve out of the station which trains could negotiate easily and without looking wildly unrealistic.

Now we had one station set up, an open frame section for a viaduct and embankment scene and a matching 6ft x 2ft board for a second station to be built on. But that didn't work for us either. Having mocked up some of the track arrangement the two stations felt much too close together, particularly for a layout set during the time of the Beeching cuts. What this line needed was a purpose greater than passenger traffic – a reason that it would be kept open and in good health. ➤➤

Mocking up the baseboards for Shortley Bridge and Felton Cement Works allowed our ideas to flow and changes to be made during the early stages of construction. Reformatting them at this point was a very simple process as the boards were only held together with G-clamps.

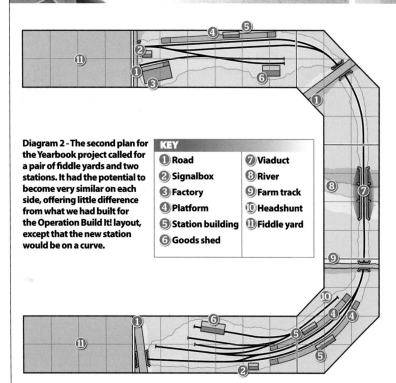

Diagram 2 - The second plan for the Yearbook project called for a pair of fiddle yards and two stations. It had the potential to become very similar on each side, offering little difference from what we had built for the Operation Build It! layout, except that the new station would be on a curve.

KEY	
① Road	⑦ Viaduct
② Signalbox	⑧ River
③ Factory	⑨ Farm track
④ Platform	⑩ Headshunt
⑤ Station building	⑪ Fiddle yard
⑥ Goods shed	

Concrete ideas

I must admit at this point that I have always had an interest in cement traffic. Distinctive wagons like the Prestwin and Presflo have always caught my eye while the white dust of cement powder is a great feature to model through weathering.

A rake of 24 Presflo wagons has been seen operating as a bulk flow on previous *Hornby Magazine* layouts including Bay Street Mk II, Bolsover and Twelve Trees Junction. Parts of the rake ran on Berrybridge too.

With such a large fleet available ideas started bubbling – and a quick trip to our storage container came up with a couple of Hornby Skaledale cement silos that we could use as the basis for mocking up a cement works.

The track layout was sketched out, laying points and yard lengths of track out on the baseboard and all of sudden we had a layout which had a purpose and all the ingredients of becoming an enjoyable and entertaining exhibition layout too.

However, cement works need buildings – lots of them. Half an hour's research later and we were staring at exactly what we needed to develop the cement works – the Walthers Valley Cement kit distributed in the UK by Gaugemaster.

Plan, planned

Now that we had a complete scheme in mind it was simply a case of building it – and building it right. We decided on DCC control from the outset with the intention that everything running on the layout will be DCC sound fitted. That gives us a few challenges, but some great projects too as one of the diesels we are particularly keen to have operating on the layout is the Class 17 Type 1 Bo-Bo.

As a DCC layout we also wanted all track to be live at all times so sound fitted locomotives can be left ticking over in sidings and loops adding to the ambience of the layout. This adds to the wiring but the end result is a totally realistic layout when it comes to operation.

From what started as a collection of possible ideas which didn't quite meet our total satisfaction, the natural evolution of this project has brought with it a new and interesting direction which we are sure will create both an eye catching and enjoyable layout to operate and we can't wait to set it up at the Warley National Model Railway Exhibition in November 2014 where it will make its public exhibition debut… ∎

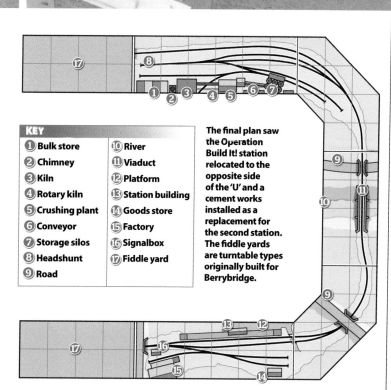

KEY	
① **Bulk store**	⑩ **River**
② **Chimney**	⑪ **Viaduct**
③ **Kiln**	⑫ **Platform**
④ **Rotary kiln**	⑬ **Station building**
⑤ **Crushing plant**	⑭ **Goods store**
⑥ **Conveyor**	⑮ **Factory**
⑦ **Storage silos**	⑯ **Signalbox**
⑧ **Headshunt**	⑰ **Fiddle yard**
⑨ **Road**	

The final plan saw the Operation Build It! station relocated to the opposite side of the 'U' and a cement works installed as a replacement for the second station. The fiddle yards are turntable types originally built for Berrybridge.

Building the BASEB

A LAYOUT like Shortley Bridge has to be built with a number of criteria in mind. Most importantly the baseboards have to be strong and sturdy and, being an exhibition layout, they also need to be light enough to be transported and of similar configurations to allow easy packing for loading into vans.

An example of the exact opposite to this is Topley Dale which was built for *Hornby Magazine Yearbook No. 5*. This layout was designed to be a 'home' based model which would only be dismantled if we moved locations. It attended one exhibition – the Warley National Model Railway Exhibition in November 2013 – but it isn't going to visit any more shows as none of the baseboards are of matching sizes which makes it very difficult to transport.

Shortley Bridge on the other hand will only be set up at exhibitions, except for when it is brought into the workshop for maintenance. That means that the design of the baseboards is critical in how they go together when assembled - and when it is stored or in transit.

With all that in mind there are three types of baseboard to make up the layout – a pair of 6ft x 2ft solid top baseboards which form the station and cement works areas. These will pack together face to face for transport. Then there are two corner boards each measuring 4ft x 3ft in total which will again pack face to face, and finally there is the viaduct board which measures 4ft x 2ft and which will be packed on its own due to the depth of the scenery.

There is a possibility that a new fiddle yard will be built for the layout and this will be designed so that it has matching shape boards to those across the viaducts scene for ease of packing.

All of the woodwork for Shortley Bridge is based around 9mm plywood for the baseboard »

WHAT WE USED		
PRODUCT	**SUPPLIER**	**PURPOSE**
9mm plywood	DIY stores	Baseboard top
69mm x 18mm planed timber	DIY stores	Baseboard frame
3.5 x 35mm woodscrews	DIY stores	Fitting tops to frames
4.0 x 40mm woodscrews	DIY stores	Fitting frames together
M6, 60mm coach bolts	DIY stores	Bolting boards together
M6, 40mm washers	DIY stores	Bolting boards together
M6 wing nuts	DIY stores	Bolting boards together

Building the baseboards for Shortley Bridge presented new challenges with a long open frame section to create the valley base. **MIKE WILD** explains how the new baseboards were built and the design criteria involved.

OARDS

tops and 69mm x 18mm planed softwood for the baseboard sides, ends and cross braces. This is a tried and tested method in the *Hornby Magazine* workshop and means we can assemble strong, rigid baseboards quickly and efficiently.

To start the process we built the second of the 6ft x 2ft solid top baseboards. The first was already built for the Operation Build It! station, so all we had to do was replicate the same steps to create the new board.

More complex were the corner and viaduct boards which had the frames built first before fitting the 9mm plywood surface. The corners of these were braced with triangles of plywood to increase their strength and ensure they were square while risers for the trackbed were cut from further sections of 69mm x 18mm softwood.

The boards are supported on trestles built for previous layouts which are assembled from 69mm x 18mm softwood screwed and glued together. This method of support makes layout assembly straightforward and reduces

BUILDING SOLID TOP BASEBOARDS

A A pre-cut piece of 1,827mm x 606mm – equal to 6ft x 2ft – 9mm plywood was used for the solid top baseboard. Four lengths of 69mm x 18mm timber are also needed to make the baseboard frame. The remaining pieces were cut at a DIY store from an 8ft x 4ft sheet.

B We started by measuring two pieces of planed timber for the sides of the frame. Mark a line across the width of the timber 1,827mm from the end using a tri-square for accuracy.

C Having marked the two side pieces the redundant ends can be cut off using either a jigsaw or a handsaw. Take care when using these tools to ensure a straight cut across the timber.

D With the ends of the side timbers cleaned up with sandpaper they can be fitted to the top. Using 3.5 x 35mm long screws the two sides of the frame were attached to the plywood top using an electric screwdriver.

E To make the end timbers for the frame, measure the space between the two outer timbers carefully at each end. We have found that the distance usually varies by a couple of millimetres from the original cutting of the plywood top.

BUILDING OPEN FRAME BASEBOARDS

1 To begin work on the open frame baseboards, the first stage was to map out the alignment of the trackbed. This was most important for the corner boards, which started out as sheets of 9mm plywood measuring 4ft x 3ft. Note the marking for which areas are to be cut away to reduce the overall size and weight of the board.

2 Having established where the board would drop away we built up a separate assembly from 69mm x 18mm softwood to form the front of the frame. The corners were braced with triangles of 9mm plywood and a single riser added to support the trackbed.

the number of bolts required to hold it all together – but it does mean remembering more equipment when it comes to exhibitions.

To join the baseboards M6 bolts with oversize washers and wing nuts were used throughout with 60mm long bolts through the majority of the boards. The only difference is on the viaduct section where 100mm long M6 bolts have been used for the upper bolt position so that they reach through the four layers of timber.

Much of the design work for the open frame baseboards evolved as the project and our ideas did, but the step by step guide with this feature shows the highlights of what is involved in building baseboards of both solid top and open frame designs. ■

TOOLS – BASEBOARD CONSTRUCTION
● Tape measure
● Tri-square
● Pencil/pen
● Jigsaw/handsaw
● Screwdriver (electric or manual)

F Having measured and cut the end pieces they can be pushed into place and fixed to the outer frame timbers with screws. It will make this job easier if you drill a pilot hole through the side timber ends to accept the screws and save splitting the wood.

G To support the centre of the baseboard two cross braces were cut to length from 69mm x 18mm timber. They were marked up using a tri-square, tape measure and pencil before being cut to length. Positioning of these is important to avoid conflicts with motor point installations in the future.

H Before fitting the cross braces three 8mm diameter holes were drilled at each end of each brace for wires to be fed through. Doing this now is easier than trying to wrestle a drill in between the framework from underneath. 3.5 x 35mm screws were used to fix the cross braces to the baseboard frame sides.

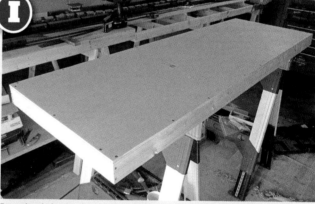

I To complete the baseboard, screws were added through the baseboard surface into the end and cross braces to provide a rigid and sturdy base for the layout. This model will be supported by a pair of our standard trestles, but could equally be supported by drawers or simpler straight legs.

3 With the front of the frame assembled the freshly cut baseboard top was offered up to ensure it was going to fit as planned.

4 The rest of the baseboard frame for the corner boards was then assembled in a 'ladder' style to ensure that all areas of the surface were fully supported.

BUILDING OPEN FRAME BASEBOARDS

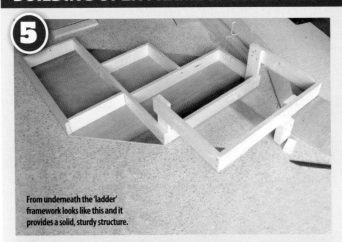

5 From underneath the 'ladder' framework looks like this and it provides a solid, sturdy structure.

6 Satisfied that everything fitted as planned the baseboard top was screwed onto the frame and work started on the second matching corner board.

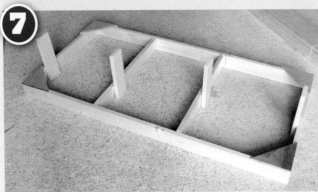

7 Next the viaduct baseboard was tackled. This board is entirely open frame in its construction. Having measured out all the parts and cut them to size to form a 4ft x 2ft baseboard all the components were laid out in a dry run to check it all fits.

8 The outer frame was then screwed together and braced with triangles of 9mm plywood on each corner.

9 The centre braces were then fitted, ensuring each one was at 90° to the frame followed by the risers to support the trackbed.

10 The completed frame was then lined up with one of the corner boards to check it was built to the correct height and dimensions one last time.

16 The final arrangement of the baseboards creates a 9ft x 12ft scenic area which extends to 13ft x 12ft when the fiddle yards are bolted on.

11

The trackbed for the open frame board was cut from a sheet of 9mm plywood using a handsaw for accuracy.

12 Finally the trackbed was screwed to the risers, completing the final baseboard for Shortley Bridge.

14 ...and the simple solution was to cut a fillet of 9mm plywood to support the track around the bend. This was marked with a pencil and then cut to fit.

13 Having built and assembled the baseboards, and subsequently changed their arrangement (see Introduction on pages 10-15) we found that the alignment of the track went off the previously planned route...

15 With a suitable length of 69mm x 18mm timber underneath, the newly added corner fillet will support the track perfectly. A second fillet was inserted on the opposite corner too.

BRANCH LINE *variety*

The branch line terminus is almost a railway modelling cliché, but in real life there was much more to single track railways than simple tank engine and single coach train, as **EVAN GREEN-HUGHES** explains.

Ex-LYR '2P' 2-4-2T 50647 waits to leave Horwich with the branch train on June 6 1958. David Hepburne-Scott/ Rail Archive Stephenson

BRANCH LINES have always been a popular subject for railway modellers. A simple terminus or passing station is more readily accommodated in a small amount of space than a double track or bigger main line. Most single track railways were populated by short passenger trains or a locomotive pulling a few wagons, an arrangement which can be realistically modelled in even the smallest of rooms.

So popular has been this type of layout that it is difficult to find a model railway exhibition which does not have at least one on show, and the most popular by far represent the quintessential Great Western Railway (GWR) branch, with those of other companies trailing along in a distant second place.

While there are advantages in modelling the typical branch, there are disadvantages too, not least because most lines of this type had very little variation in either locomotives or rolling stock. All bar the most lightly used branch might have seen a number of different types of locomotive while the same passenger train would be seen shuttling up and down the line all day with perhaps the odd visit from time to time from a through secondary train.

Of course, most of the classic branch lines were closed down in the 1950s and 1960s so those who wish to model a more modern scene find that they need to look elsewhere for inspiration.

REALITY CHECK

The Whitby-Scarborough line was famous for its viaducts and dramatic views and was single track throughout. Ex-NER 'A8' 4-6-2T 69867 climbs Ravenscar bank with a Whitby-Scarborough train in September 1954. Gordon Hepburn/Rail Archive Stephenson.

Modelling sense

The advantages of modelling a single track line far outweigh the disadvantages. Track layouts at stations tend to be much simpler, connections to depots and yards require less space and where there is plain track only half as much width is needed. With this in mind it's worth looking to see whether there are other single track lines which offer a variation on the traditional themes.

In the early days of the railways many lines were single track. Wagonways from colliery to **»**

Branch and single line routes attracted an impressive variety of traffic. On April 18 1963 Ivatt '2MT' 2-6-0 46509 with a Cambrian coast train near Towyn which includes two BR Mk 1 sleeping cars. David Hepburne-Scott/Rail Archive Stephenson.

canal were usually only provided with one line of rails and this pattern was followed when many of the first public railways were built.

It wasn't long, though, before traffic demand was such that one track was provided for trains running in each direction with early examples including the Stockton and Darlington and the Liverpool and Manchester Railways. Double track was used for most of the major parts of the network but some routes were laid as single track, though sometimes with bridges and tunnels built to accommodate future expansion. Not surprisingly many lines were never upgraded, including the Wear Valley Railway in County Durham and the Clayton West Branch in Yorkshire which remained single track until the end.

Once the trunk routes had been constructed attention turned to serving more remote parts of the country, with most of these places being served by single track branch lines. It would be easy to think that this meant a few miles of single line served by a handful of trains but in reality some of these branches were tens of miles long and carried the sort of traffic you would normally associate with a full-blown main line.

A main line branch?

If you're put off buying one of Hornby's new 'P2' 2-8-2 express locomotives because of their main line purpose and think that one would look out of place on a single track, you might be encouraged to discover that they *are* appropriate as there were single track sections from Edinburgh to Aberdeen. These huge locomotives even had tablet exchange apparatus fitted for the single line section from Usan to Montrose South, which included a single track viaduct over the Montrose Esk Basin.

Although this was only a short section of the Aberdeen route, the Highland Main Line from Perth to Inverness included many miles

of single track which has seen everything from fast overnight expresses to intermodal trains over the years. This line was even a major strategic route during the First World War and saw an endless procession of coal and ammunition trains.

Further west the West Highland Line to Fort William and Mallaig was single track throughout, but this route had more of the atmosphere of a typical branch line, with small stations surrounded by spectacular scenery. However there were some heavy trains running this way, too, and double-headed 2-6-0s or 4-6-0s were commonplace before diesels came. In the early morning and late evening there were the long 'sleeper' trains (which still run today) and even well into the diesel era there were freight trains conveying logs and also aluminium products from the smelter near Fort William.

The West Highland extension from Fort William to Mallaig again is a branch line, but in this case over 40 miles long and which once had express goods trains conveying freshly landed fish running along it. With its steep gradients and severe curves this line would provide plenty of opportunities for modellers, particularly those who follow today's scene for the regular Class 156 Diesel Multiple Units (DMUs) share the route with timetabled steam services and special excursion trains, which throw up even more variation in motive power.

Anglian reflections

Many of the routes through rural East Anglia were laid out for single track, yet there were busy stations and junctions which saw traffic much heavier than might have been expected. The area had a complex system of lines right up to the Beeching era, many of which saw intensive holiday traffic at weekends and very heavy agricultural traffic at other times of the year.

This area was one of the first to have diesel

Above: **On the North Cornwall Railway lines Bulleid 'Pacifics' rubbed shoulders with 'M7' 0-4-4Ts and 'T9' 4-4-0s at the head of short passenger trains to reach coastal outposts. On May 18 1959 'Battle of Britain' 4-6-2 34072 *257 Squadron* propels the stock for the up 'Atlantic Coast Express' into Ilfracombe station.** Ken Cook/Rail Archive Stephenson.

Right: **The Southern Region had many branch lines and developed push-pull trains where the driver could operate the locomotive from a cab in the leading carriage to assist in branch line operation. Drummond 'M7' 0-4-4T 30029 arrives at Rowfant with the Three Bridges to East Grinstead branch train on March 3 1963 formed of a Maunsell push-pull set.** Mike Fox/Rail Archive Stephenson.

railcars and would allow the modeller to run these alongside some truly distinctive steam locomotives, such as the 'D11' 4-4-0s – a model soon to be released by Hornby. Unlike the routes in Scotland most of East Anglia's branch lines were closed during the Beeching period but some did survive into the British Rail era and even today there are long branches, although most now are only operated by Class 153 or 156 DMUs.

Crossing the country

Worth consideration when looking for modelling inspiration are the secondary routes which criss-crossed the country but which were built as single lines to save money. One of the most famous of these was the East-West route of the Cockermouth, Keswick and Penrith Railway which threaded its way through some of the most spectacular scenery in the country as it made its way through the Lake District to the coast.

Although this looked like a typical branch line with its small and perfectly manicured stations it was in fact for much of its life a trunk route carrying heavy freight, particularly coal and minerals, on their way to and from the Cumbrian coast to Teeside and which were mixed in with local trains, usually worked by 2-4-0 or 0-6-0 engines of London & North Western Railway origin.

The route also saw a lot of tourist traffic which would give the modeller chance to introduce express stock and this tradition carried on right until BR days when it was not uncommon to see long trains of new Mk 1 coaches hauled by 'Black Fives'. Only the stump of the line between Keswick and Penrith outlasted the Beeching era and this was almost entirely populated with DMUs by that time, the railways having thrown in the towel as regards most of the other traffic and unfortunately even this piece of line is no longer with us today.

Welsh wizardry

Wales also had its fair share of long distance branch lines. Those in the valleys surrounding Cardiff were about as far away from the stereotype as you could get for, although they were single track, they carried vast quantities of coal from the collieries in the valleys, through Cardiff and onwards to the docks. Traffic was dominated by 0-6-2Ts which plodded up and down with endless strings of mineral wagons but there were also the usual 0-6-0PTs and GWR 2-6-2Ts on local passenger workings as well as a range of locomotives from the independent companies which operated many of the routes until the 1923 grouping.

Although an attractive proposition in some

ways, a model of one of the valley routes would present a problem in that many of the trains were very long and would require quite a large layout to accommodate them. Even comparatively recently there was considerable coal traffic with HAA hoppers and the like being worked by Class 37s to and from the valley pits, at first mixed in with Class 116 suburban DMUs and later with Class 150 'Sprinters' and Class 143 'Pacers'.

The principality was also host to a number of secondary single track lines which, while rural in character, carried substantial and varied traffic. The route from Shrewsbury through Welshpool and over Talerddig Summit had something of a branch line atmosphere yet the trains which traversed it included many of considerable length, particularly during the holiday season. The onwards routes from Dovey Junction to Aberystwyth and Pwllheli were also single with the latter containing many miles of track running alongside the sea.

These routes survived the Beeching cuts and offer modellers of the post-steam era the chance to model a branch line. The BR blue era would be particularly interesting as at that time the line still possessed its full Victorian infrastructure but played host to 10 and 11 coach trains each weekend, hauled by Class 31s and Class 37s. Also prominent in the area ➤➤

The Lyme Regis branch had a unique requirement for powerful locomotives capable of negotiating tight curves and the Adams radial tanks were the answer. Radial 4-4-2T 30582 arrives at Lyme Regis with the 1.38pm from Axminster on September 1 1958. *Ken Cook/Rail Archive Stephenson.*

were Class 25s which found use on local goods and, of course, DMUs. Nowadays things are not quite so interesting as Class 158s predominate and the only locomotive action comes from a handful of Network Rail Class 37s which have been fitted with the necessary European Train Control System signalling equipment. Nevertheless there has been steam in the recent past and it can't be ruled out for the future.

During the real steam era these lines hosted a useful variation of Great Western locomotives, in particular the 'Dukedogs' 4-4-0s (the subject of a wonderful recent model by Bachmann in 'OO' gauge) and the 'Manor' 4-6-0s, but there were also many other designs, both tender and tank locomotives, to be seen. Towards the end London Midland Region classes took over and so it's possible to have quite a big stud of locomotives on a branch line of this type.

The same is true of coaching stock because the holiday expresses came from all over the country and the line therefore saw unlikely sights such as Gresley teaks from the London

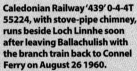

Caledonian Railway '439' 0-4-4T 55224, with stove-pipe chimney, runs beside Loch Linnhe soon after leaving Ballachulish with the branch train back to Connel Ferry on August 26 1960.
David Hepburne-Scott/Rail Archive Stephenson.

and North Eastern Railway and Stanier suburban coaches from the London Midland & Scottish, all mixed with the home grown GWR designs.

The island line

Although it was a self-contained system, the 55-mile Isle of Wight Railway offers the modeller another way of producing a branch line with a different character altogether. In steam days there was a fleet of ancient 'O2' 0-4-4Ts operating what was essentially an entire railway network in miniature. The island had its own junctions, main and branch lines, ferry ports and harbours which resulted in a level of service which was not found on many conventional branch lines anywhere.

The geography of the island meant that there was intensive goods traffic which was, like the passenger service, accommodated in vehicles which had been pensioned off from the mainland and were often many years beyond their sell-by date. The system had a number of delightful stations too which would make

'J25' 0-6-0 65700 arrives at Wheldrake with a Cliffe Common to York Layerthorpe goods on September 8 1952. Stan Garth/Rail Archive Stephenson.

a good subject, particularly those which saw regular passing moves, such as Sandown or Shanklin.

Unfortunately modernisation has not been kind to the Isle of Wight and retired tube trains now provide the regular passenger service, while an idea of what the system used to be like can be gained from a visit to the Isle of Wight Steam Railway which is based on part of the Ryde to Newport line. However a location such as Smallbrook Junction where a single track steam-worked heritage line joins an electrified route populated by former London Underground trains offers much of interest along with a distinctive setting.

The Isle of Wight had a number of terminus stations which were larger than the average but even if you've space for a main line layout, some of the larger stations on the island and elsewhere offer massive potential. Even Mallaig, at the end of the West Highland Line, was quite a large undertaking as it provided accommodation for the considerable fish traffic which originated from there and Aberystwyth in mid Wales was on a scale which would have benefitted the end of a main line. Sadly today this coastal terminus is now a single platform terminus with the narrow gauge Vale of Rheidol Railway next to it, although the spectacular station buildings remain.

One advantage of modelling such a terminus is that the approach track arrangement tends to be simpler and is thus easier to design into the space available. Those looking for a challenge could do no better than Inverness which has a triangular layout serving single track routes which run both north and south, although in the vicinity of the station it's hard to tell that this is the case due to the complicated setup of the departure and arrival lines.

Modelling the heritage scene

While there has been a steady increase in the number of heritage railways operating in the UK since enthusiasts took over the Talyllyn Railway in 1952 there has not been a corresponding increase in models of preservation sites – which does seem curious »

It's not what we think of first when it comes to a branch line scene, but the Highland Main Line featured long single track sections and long trains. Pickersgill '3P' 4-4-0 54482 pilots Stanier 'Black Five' 44924 two miles north of Carr Bridge on the climb to Slochd summit with a northbound coal train in August 1959.
W.J. Verden Anderson/Rail Archive Stephenson.

The Ashburton branch is hailed as the quintessential Great Western branch line. GWR '14XX' 0-4-2T 1427, still with GWR on its tanks, waits to leave Ashburton with the auto train for Totnes on June 26 1952. Stan Garth/Rail Archive Stephenson.

given the scope for genuine 'anything goes' operation.

Many of these railways are based on former branch lines but now see services at a level which would have been unthinkable in their heyday. In addition there is a variety of traction and rolling stock which would never have been seen at any point in history. Some of these railways are also connected to the national network, offering the chance for steam or diesel hauled railtours to bring extra variety to a potential layout. A major line such as the Severn Valley Railway retains the appearance of a Great Western branch but on a typical day will host full length sets of rolling stock from the Great Western, London Midland & Scottish, London and North Eastern and British Railways which can be hauled by anything from an 0-6-0PT to new-build 'A1' 4-6-2 60163 *Tornado*. The line has also played host to Class 150 and similar modern DMUs and often sees special trains working through from destinations on the national network.

Lines such as the Weardale Railway, meanwhile, have operated timetabled freight, producing the incongruous sight of a heritage DMU passing a Class 66 diesel on coal hoppers on preservation infrastructure. Another variation to this theme is the Midland Railway Butterley which plays host to a number of Network Rail Multiple Purpose Vehicles, which can often be seen operating on its line for training purposes.

There are, then, many alternatives to the popular GWR branch line terminus should you not be a follower of that company. With a little planning and careful selection of prototype you'll be surprised at the sheer variety, interest and personality of Britain's multitude of branch lines, both past and present. ■

Laying the PERMAN

TO BUILD A MODEL RAILWAY properly you should start with a trackplan – right? Well, not necessarily. Like many of our projects the trackplan for Shortley Bridge and Felton Cement Works evolved during the layout's construction. Naturally we had ideas in mind, but not everything works out as you might imagine.

The starting point for this project was modification of the Operation Build It! terminus station leading to the removal of the pointwork for the run-round loop, buffer stops and ballast to extend both lines adjacent to the platform into through lines.

Fortunately the layout had been built with future extension in mind, although exactly how that extension would take place was open to debate until we set about physical work. Removal of the original track was relatively straightforward, but had to be done with care to avoid damaging the plain track of the original loops and the surrounding scenery. We only took out the headshunts and associated points leaving the plain track in situ. However, this also meant removing all the original ballasting by carefully scraping it away with a chisel and finally taking out the original cork. The whole area then had to cleaned up using a vacuum cleaner to remove the remaining debris. Even when modifying an existing layout it is essential to work from a smooth and clean base for the best running properties.

Finescale look

The Operation Build It! layout was built with Peco code 75 track and the extension work to create Shortley Bridge and Felton Cement Works uses products from the same range. Having cleared the area we allocated a large radius curved point to form the junction for the loops at Shortley Bridge station. The loops consist of a passenger line and goods line and both will be bi-directional.

After leaving the station the trackplan is quite simple – a single line continues on around a curve, under a road bridge, across a viaduct and under a second road bridge before beginning the curve on the approach to the cement works. All of this was laid using flexible track which allows for smooth flowing curves along the route of the railway.

The cement works trackplan developed on the baseboard and started with a rough mock-up of a potential arrangement working back from the headshunt to the main line connection. There were two important factors to ensure with this – first that the headshunt was long enough and secondly that the loops were long enough to accommodate

TOOLS

- Minidrill with cutting disc or hacksaw
- Pin hammer
- Pin vice
- 1mm drill bit
- Pliers
- Electric drill and 8mm drill bit
- Wire cutters
- Wire strippers

the train lengths we had in mind. This meant that the headshunt was measured out to take a Class 08 diesel shunter and four 'Presflo' cement wagons while the loops will hold nine wagons and a brake van without a locomotive – on arrival the train engine would always be removed anyway, giving access to the cement works shunters to move the formation into the correct sidings.

The connection to the main line is via a large radius curved left-hand point which links into a second matching point to open the two loops. These are to handle incoming and outgoing cement trains. Behind these loops there are two long sidings – one for storage and the furthest back for cement loading. To make operation more interesting there is a third siding accessed from the loading line and an internal track which branches off and disappears through the backscene. The intention here is that incoming coal traffic will be transported onto this line to reach the furnaces for the cement works.

The main line alongside the cement works remains as a single line and again all of the plain track has been laid with Peco code 75 flexible track.

Joints and electrics

At the baseboard joints the track needs to be cut to allow Shortley Bridge to be a portable layout. However, it is no good just cutting the track – it needs anchoring to the baseboard to ensure that it is correctly aligned every time it is assembled. To do this sleepers were cut away from the rails either side of each baseboard joint and replaced with copper-clad sleepers. At angled joins more sleepers were cut away and a series of copper-clad sleepers were laid across the baseboard joint. Once pinned to the board the rails were soldered to the copper strips before the rails were cut to make the joint. At the angled joins the rails and sleepers were cut through in line with the baseboard joint.

Wiring for Shortley Bridge follows the same principles as the Operation Build It! station. All of the track is live all of the time to make the most of Digital Command Control operation and the »

A Class 17 departs
Felton Cement
Works with a rake
of Presflos.

With the baseboards built the next phase of development for Shortley Bridge is laying the track and fitting electrical connections. **MIKE WILD** shows how it is done.

ENT WAY

All the track for Shortley Bridge and Felton Cement Works is from the Peco code 75 range. A Bachmann Class 25 passes the cement works with a ballast train on the newly laid main line.

sound fitted locomotives that will run on the layout. This has been achieved by isolating the inner rails of each side of a point at its toe end and adding an extra feed to power the isolated rail. The feed wires are seven strand multi-core wire in different colours which are taken back to connector blocks which, in turn, are then connected to the main power bus wire. The main bus wire, which acts like a ring main in a house by providing a main cable to supply the rest of the layout, is made from 16 strand multi-core wire which reduces the potential for power drops.

At each baseboard joint only two wires are required to conduct electricity and DCC signals to the next board, as the only connection is for the main power bus. This is connected through 6amp plug-in terminal blocks suitable for high power use with the large diameter cable used for the power bus.

Model railway electrics have the potential to sound complex, but in fact whether you are building an analogue or digital layout the majority of the wiring is simple repetition of the same circuit. The best advice we can offer is to be methodical, take your time and colour code everything – that way you will always know where each wire is headed.

The final essential part of the track laying and wiring stage is to thoroughly test the whole layout before moving on any further. Check every connection, check every track, check that all the

WHAT WE USED		
PRODUCT	**MANUFACTURER**	**CAT NO.**
Code 75 flexible track	www.peco-uk.com	SL-100F
Code 75 medium right point	www.peco-uk.com	SL-E195
Code 75 medium left point	www.peco-uk.com	SL-E196
Code 75 large curved right point	www.peco-uk.com	SL-E186
Code 75 large curved left point	www.peco-uk.com	SL-E187
Code 75 rail joiners	www.peco-uk.com	SL-110
Code 75 insulated rail joiners	www.peco-uk.com	SL-111
Track pins	www.peco-uk.com	ST-280
Cork, 1/16in thick, 36in x 24in	www.gaugemaster.com	GM130
Bufferstops	www.peco-uk.com	Sl-40
Matt acrylic spray paint, brown	www.humbrol.com	29
Geoscenics 'N' gauge limestone wagon load	www.hornbymagazine.com	MOD19
Geoscenics 'N' gauge ballast wagon load	www.hornbymagazine.com	MOD22
Geoscenics track/ballast dirt	www.geoscenics.co.uk	TG50
7/0.2 multi-core wire in two colours	www.rapidonline.com	Various
16/0.2 multi-core bell wire	www.rapidonline.com	Various
6A plug in terminal block	www.rapidonline.com	21-4278
Masking tape	DIY stores	Various

points work - and with a variety of locomotives and rolling stock too. Check the headshunt lengths, check the loop lengths and everything else you can as modifications after the next stage will be much more difficult.

Weathering and ballasting

To complete the track for the extension it needed to be weathered and ballasted to match that of

the original station. The starting point for this was to cover the point blades with strips of masking tape to ensure that no paint could enter this important area during the weathering process.

Once this was done weathering took a matter of minutes by using an aerosol can of Humbrol No 29 to tone down the rail sides, sleepers and immediate vicinity of the track. One area was most complex through – the Operation Build It!

station. Here care had to be taken to fully mask the platform and existing ballasted track before it was weathered. The No 29 aerosol was used again to complete this area.

Finishing up work on the track is ballasting. We needed the ballast to match that on the original Operation Build It! station board, so the materials we used were Geoscenics 'N' gauge limestone wagon load and 'N' gauge ballast from the *Hornby*

Magazine wagon load kit range. These two grades of stone were mixed together in varying quantities and then spread onto the track formation loose. A 1in paintbrush was then used to carefully move the ballast into place, being careful to avoid filling the point mechanism. Next, model oil was added around the point blades and mechanism to repel the glue before PVA glue diluted 50:50 with water and mixed with Geoscenics track dirt paint and

a drop of detergent was applied to the loose laid ballast. To assist the glue in flowing into the ballast it was wetted with a water mister containing water and a drop of detergent first.

After the ballast had been left to set thoroughly overnight all the track needed to be cleaned and tested again which then allowed us to move onto the next stages of the project - creating the landscape and scenery… ■

LAYING THE PERMANENT WAY FOR SHORTLEY BRIDGE

The track laying process began by removing the points and headshunt from the station. Track pins were removed first before a chisel was used to carefully lift the track, cork and ballast.

Having removed the track the debris needs to be removed with a vacuum cleaner. It is essential to have a smooth and clean base onto which new track can be laid.

LAYING THE PERMANENT WAY FOR SHORTLEY BRIDGE

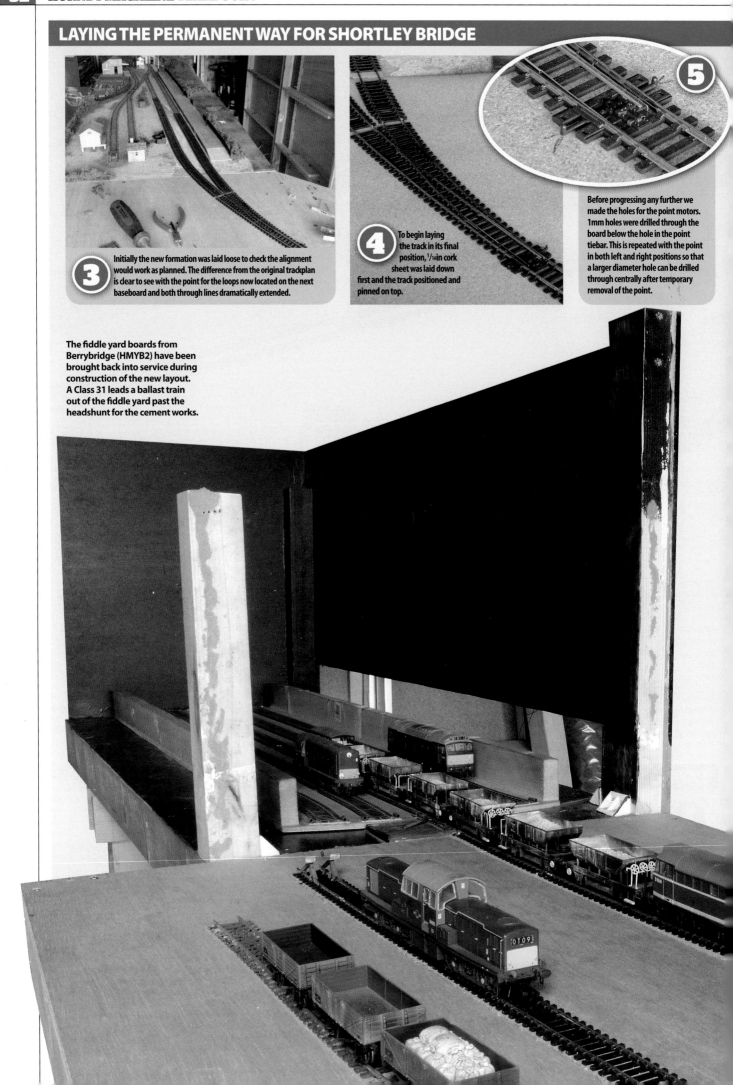

3 Initially the new formation was laid loose to check the alignment would work as planned. The difference from the original trackplan is clear to see with the point for the loops now located on the next baseboard and both through lines dramatically extended.

4 To begin laying the track in its final position, ¹/₁₆in cork sheet was laid down first and the track positioned and pinned on top.

5

Before progressing any further we made the holes for the point motors. 1mm holes were drilled through the board below the hole in the point tiebar. This is repeated with the point in both left and right positions so that a larger diameter hole can be drilled through centrally after temporary removal of the point.

The fiddle yard boards from Berrybridge (HMYB2) have been brought back into service during construction of the new layout. A Class 31 leads a ballast train out of the fiddle yard past the headshunt for the cement works.

6 Triangular marks at each side of the point help locate the 1mm holes created in Step 5 once the point has been removed.

7 With the point removed an 8mm hole can be drilled through the baseboard with an electric drill. Be careful to avoid conflicts with baseboard frames – we had to reposition this point to avoid the motor position clashing with the frame.

8 With the hole drilled and the surface cleaned up the point is reinstated for the final time and the cork sheet trimmed back to the edges of the sleepers.

9 On the main line the flexible track is joined together using metal rail joiners and then laid over cork sheet which is wider than immediately needed.

10 Using a craft knife with a sharp blade, the cork is cut away at the sleeper edges for a neat finish.

11 The final result is track which sits neatly on a cork base. The cork creates a 'shoulder' for later ballasting and helps make the track look more realistic.

12 Planning for the cement works trackplan was carried out on the baseboards. Here we are mocking up the arrangement and checking that the siding lengths we need are possible.

13 The completed cement works track layout offers plenty of operational potential and will soon feature a full complement of buildings too.

LAYING THE PERMANENT WAY FOR SHORTLEY BRIDGE

At the baseboard joints the track needs to be anchored to the baseboard to support it during transport and also to ensure that it always lines up when the layout is assembled. To do this plastic sleepers are cut away from the rails either side of the baseboard joint and strips of copper-clad strip are inserted in their place.

1mm holes are drilled in each corner for the copper strip so that they can be pinned to the baseboard. At the same time a notch is made in the copper surface of the strip on both sides to isolate the two rails and stop short circuits.

Next the rails are soldered to the copper-clad strips, hence the need to notch the copper surface as in Step 15, to secure the rails at the baseboard joint.

Using a cutting disc in a mini drill the rails and, where necessary due to their angle, the copper-clad strips, are cut through to complete the baseboard joint.

Having cut the tracks wiring is now required in certain positions to bring power to the rails. 2mm holes are drilled in the correct locations and wires are soldered to the rail sides after stripping back 15mm of insulation.

Once soldered to the rails, the wires can be pulled through the holes in the baseboard for a neat appearance, minimising their visual impact.

To make the whole trackplan live takes extra wiring. Each point has insulated rail joiners on the inner rails at the toe end which allows a separate wire to be soldered on to provide permanent power to each section of track. The green and white wires are coloured coded to left and right rails.

With the track wired and tested the next phase is to weather and ballast it. Weathering starts by protecting the point blades with strips of masking tape.

The track is then weathered with an aerosol spray paint – Humbrol acrylic No 29 in this case – for a quick application and quick drying method.

At the station the area around the track had to be masked thoroughly to avoid spray paint covering the platform and previously ballasted track.

Loose ballast using a combination of Geoscenics limestone and ballast 'N' gauge wagon loads was spread over the track loose.

It was then brushed into place carefully with a 1in paint brush to prepare it for gluing.

A few drops of model oil were then applied around the point blades and mechanism to stop the glue seizing the points.

Finally the ballast was wetted with a water mister before PVA glue mixed with water to a 50:50 ratio with a drop of detergent and Geoscenics track dirt added was applied with a syringe. This was left to dry overnight before the track was cleaned and tested again.

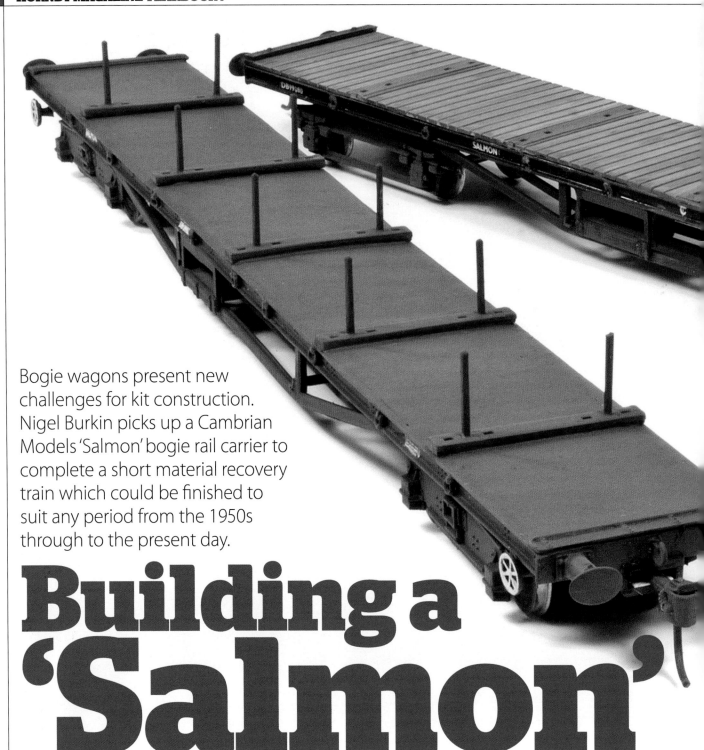

Bogie wagons present new challenges for kit construction. Nigel Burkin picks up a Cambrian Models 'Salmon' bogie rail carrier to complete a short material recovery train which could be finished to suit any period from the 1950s through to the present day.

Building a 'Salmon'

ENGINEER'S TRAFFIC came in forms including trains delivering fresh ballast, others taking dirty 'spoil' away and those which carried both fresh and old rails. In Hornby Magazine we've already shown how to build the Cambrian Models 'Sturgeon A' and 'Borail' wagons, but in this feature we'll be completing the recovery train with a pair of Cambrian Models 'Salmon' kits.

These vehicles have been long lived. The British Railways designed wagon is still used today and owes its origins to a 1940s London Midland & Scottish Railway (LMS) design of which 100 wagons were constructed. The LMS design was continued by BR to Diagram 1/640; constructed circa 1949 and 1952 and numbered DB996000-099 and DB996152-213 prior to the introduction of the BR 'Salmon'.

Of the LMS constructed 'Salmon' (actually coded 'Borail J/MD'), there were three documented types: one with low floor bolsters or plates with locating holes for stanchions; one with low bolsters and a third with taller bolsters. The BR constructed wagons were essentially the same being based on LMS Diagram 19G. Published photographs indicate that they had a wooden planked deck and no bolsters except in a few instances where low bolsters were fitted.

The LMS derived design differs from the BR 'Salmon' further in having LMS 8ft wheelbase bogies similar to coach bogies with a brake lever on one side. The wagons were unfitted and eventually coded YMO with the introduction of TOPS. They were pretty unassuming vehicles with minimal markings and black as a livery with grey weathering and ruststained wood planking. Some modifications were applied to them over the years including the fitting of ratchet tensioners and

chain boxes. A number of them were modernised with air brakes and repainted engineers yellow, surviving into the early 1990s.

The second wagon of this project is the BR 'Salmon' which was constructed between 1952 and 1961 – a perfect partner to the LMS-derived wagon. There were two basic types including Diagram 1/642 with short 5ft-6in wheelbase plateback bogies and Diagram 1/646 which were fitted with 8ft wheelbase plateback bogies. Other differences included a steel floor and a single chain box fitted as standard. They were either unfitted (YMO) or equipped with a through vacuum pipe (YMP). Many had the bolsters removed by the time TOPS codes were allocated so they could carry 60ft long track panels. When built, the wagons were painted black with white markings. It is unclear if any received olive green livery before the modernised versions were painted engineers yellow and grey. They operated »

HOW TO GUIDES

'Salmon' engineer's wagons complete the short train of rail carrying wagons being constructed for Nigel's Folkestone East layout. They are finished in plain black with white markings and weathering.

BUILDING CAMBRIAN MODELS 'SALMON' BOGIE WAGONS

1 I always start with the bogies. This is a view of the bogie and pivot components from the LMS 'Salmon'.

2 The sideframes and spacer are carefully cleaned of moulding flash and pinpoint bearings are inserted into the axle holes. A spot of superglue will hold loose ones in place.

3 Both types of plateback bogie used in the BR 'Salmon' kit and the LMS 8ft bogies are assembled the same way. Use the wheels to assist with assembly and to achieve a square bogie.

4 Bogie bearing pads are fitted with a pivot screw which is 'fixed' in the moulding. The same pivoting method is used for both kits.

throughout the BR network and could be found in almost any yard or engineers siding.

Some BR 'Salmon' were modernised with air brakes in the early 1980s, being coded YMA. The type remains in use today with the majority used to carry track panels and concrete sleepers.

Compared to the LMS design, the BR design has seen the greatest number of modifications and finding a 'typical' example is hard. There are numerous variations that could be researched for some imaginative projects including loading cranes, bolsters, inspection platforms, canopies, longitudinal timbers and tensioners supplementing and replacing the chain loops.

To overcome the maintenance issues surrounding the plateback bogies, English Welsh & Scottish Railway (EWS) started to fit modern ASF bogies to surviving wagons in 1998 creating the YWA.

The 'Salmon' continues to be an important wagon with many being adapted from YWA with new end stanchions and a centre bolster to carry track panels without strapping. Coded YKA, they have been allocated the Fishkind name 'Osprey'.

The Cambrian kit

Four 'Salmon' kits are offered by Cambrian Models. The first one of interest is the LMS design which is represented by kit C47. It can be used to build one of the LMS wagons to LMS Diagram 19E/F and G built between 1940 and 1942 together with those built by BR to Diagram 1/640.

The second kit is C27, representing the BR 50ton 'Salmon' to Diagram 1/646 with 8ft plate back bogies, the second kit to be featured in this article. A short wheelbase bogie version is also available as kit C46 which is built in the same manner and shares the same parts as C27 apart from the bogies.

Modern wagon modellers will welcome kit C88 which represents the modernised version of the BR 'Salmon' as equipped with ASF bogies. It is the fourth 'Salmon' in the range and would be appropriate for layouts dated from 1998 onwards.

The kits are composed of light grey styrene plastic easily assembled using solvent cement. There are some shared parts between the kits including the solebar moulding which is taken

from the BR 'Salmon' and applied to the LMS design too. Bogies are not complete units but have to be glued together and fitted with brass pinpoint bearings. 10.5mm diameter wheels and couplings have to be sourced to complete the kit. Ballast weight is also required to give the model some mass.

The kits are supplied with brackets allowing the use of tension lock couplings. They are fitted to the bogies and have different fixing positions for coupling position relative to the buffers to accommodate sharp curves. After all, the wagons are a scale 65ft long with the bogies inboard of the headstocks at scale 45ft centres, so buffer lock on sharp curves is a possibility if the couplings are fitted too far inboard of the buffers.

In common with all Cambrian Models kits, the tools required to successfully assemble a wagon are amongst the simplest in the toolbox. Ensure that your modelling knife has a fresh supply of blades because blunt blades can slip and damage some of the components. Consider a set of Xuron sprue cutters for removing parts from the kit sprue and remember that wet and dry abrasive paper is excellent for gently cleaning the edges of kit parts and removing mould lines. Other tools you will need will include small drills, a pin vice, files, tweezers and pliers together with painting materials.

As suggested with most wagon kit building, start with the bogies and check that they run straight and true before turning to the wagon itself. Check for moulding pips that may prevent parts from seating correctly, particularly along the bevelled join between floor and solebars. Enjoy the building process and the creation of something unique for your layout. I built both models together and found the challenge of making moulded plastic look like painted metal and wood an absorbing exercise. Total construction time was around two to three hours per kit. Painting and finishing took longer.

Painting

Unfitted and vacuum-piped 'Salmon' are simple to paint - bogies and superstructure are finished in black with simple white markings. Spraying the livery on both wagons was completed quickly after

the bearings in the bogies were protected from paint with a tiny square of masking tape – only one coat was required. The timber decking of the LMS based wagon was also painted black to pre-shade it for wood effects. Gloss varnish was applied to the solebars to help with the application of transfers after the black coat of paint had been left to dry for at least 24 hours. Numbers and codes were made up of various numerals from the Cambrian Models CT4 transfer sheet also now offered by Modelmaster Decals in waterslide format.

The deck of the BR 'Salmon' was coated with a mixture of brown rust and a spot of frame dirt colour. The wooden deck of the LMS wagon was painted grey with some planks highlighted in different shades to represent worn and weathered wood. Rust staining and grime was applied over the grey wood colour. White was applied to brake wheels and brake lever handles. A coat of varnish followed and the models together with the bogies and wheels were completed with spot rusting and a dusting of frame dirt to tone down the black livery.

Completing the train

To complete the train, I used a ready to run brake van. The Bachmann Southern Railway 25ton brake van is the perfect model to complete the set. I chose the ZTP version finished in olive green to suit a 1970s and 1980s period for which the black 'Salmon' wagons are appropriate. However, if you are modelling an earlier period or different regions there are plenty of BR bauxite liveried brake vans on the market including both BR and Southern Railway built 25ton vans. The brake was carefully weathered with bare wood planks, paint patching, rusted framing and underframe dirt colour.

Having built a handful of unfitted 'Salmon' wagons and a 'Sturgeon' for this exercise in bogie wagon kit building, it looks as if I will need a couple more to augment the train! The building of the Cambrian Models kits was a satisfying and rewarding way of adding to my engineering wagon fleet to suit the late 1970s and early 1980s part of operations on my Folkestone East layout. Such kit building leavens the diet of ready-to-run wagons and adds some very fulfilling variety to the layout. ■

A single MLV runs up the incline from Martello tunnel on its way to Ashford as a Class 33 attends to the 'Salmon' and 'Sturgeon' wagons in the yard. Many areas of the layout remain to be completed – but what's the rush?

BUILDING CAMBRIAN MODELS 'SALMON' BOGIE WAGONS

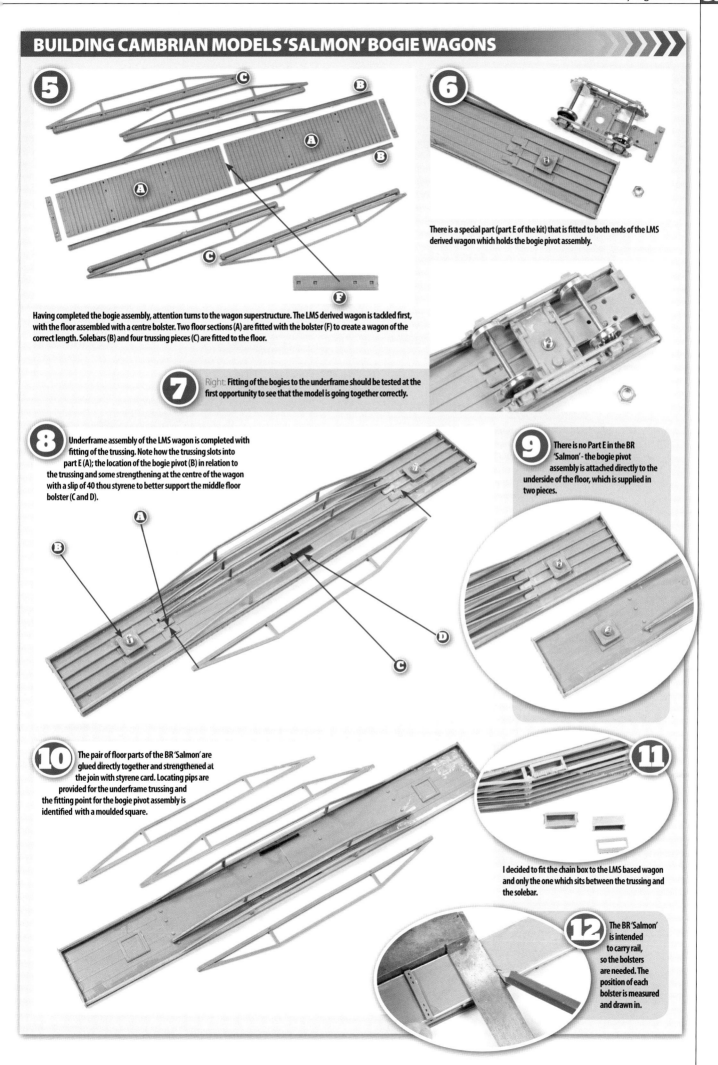

5

6 There is a special part (part E of the kit) that is fitted to both ends of the LMS derived wagon which holds the bogie pivot assembly.

Having completed the bogie assembly, attention turns to the wagon superstructure. The LMS derived wagon is tackled first, with the floor assembled with a centre bolster. Two floor sections (A) are fitted with the bolster (F) to create a wagon of the correct length. Solebars (B) and four trussing pieces (C) are fitted to the floor.

7 Right: Fitting of the bogies to the underframe should be tested at the first opportunity to see that the model is going together correctly.

8 Underframe assembly of the LMS wagon is completed with fitting of the trussing. Note how the trussing slots into part E (A); the location of the bogie pivot (B) in relation to the trussing and some strengthening at the centre of the wagon with a slip of 40 thou styrene to better support the middle floor bolster (C and D).

9 There is no Part E in the BR 'Salmon' - the bogie pivot assembly is attached directly to the underside of the floor, which is supplied in two pieces.

10 The pair of floor parts of the BR 'Salmon' are glued directly together and strengthened at the join with styrene card. Locating pips are provided for the underframe trussing and the fitting point for the bogie pivot assembly is identified with a moulded square.

11 I decided to fit the chain box to the LMS based wagon and only the one which sits between the trussing and the solebar.

12 The BR 'Salmon' is intended to carry rail, so the bolsters are needed. The position of each bolster is measured and drawn in.

BUILDING CAMBRIAN MODELS 'SALMON' BOGIE WAGONS

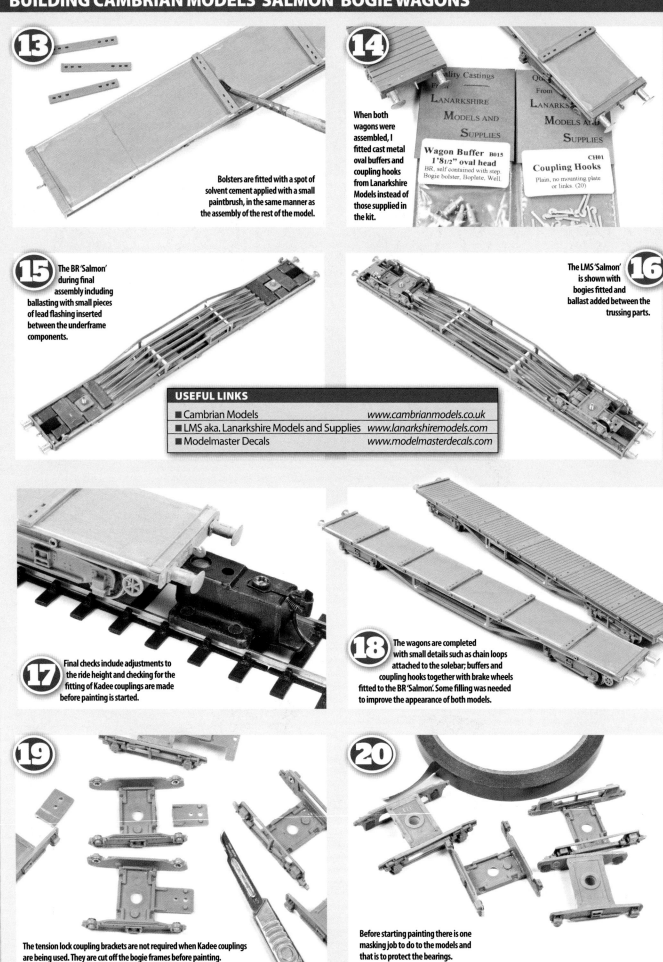

13 Bolsters are fitted with a spot of solvent cement applied with a small paintbrush, in the same manner as the assembly of the rest of the model.

14 When both wagons were assembled, I fitted cast metal oval buffers and coupling hooks from Lanarkshire Models instead of those supplied in the kit.

Quality Castings
From
Lanarkshire
Models and
Supplies
Wagon Buffer B015
1'81/2" oval head
BR, self contained with step.
Bogie bolster, Boplate, Well.

Qu...
From
Lanarks...
Models and
Supplies
CH01
Coupling Hooks
Plain, no mounting plate
or links. (20)

15 The BR 'Salmon' during final assembly including ballasting with small pieces of lead flashing inserted between the underframe components.

16 The LMS 'Salmon' is shown with bogies fitted and ballast added between the trussing parts.

USEFUL LINKS
- Cambrian Models — www.cambrianmodels.co.uk
- LMS aka. Lanarkshire Models and Supplies — www.lanarkshiremodels.com
- Modelmaster Decals — www.modelmasterdecals.com

17 Final checks include adjustments to the ride height and checking for the fitting of Kadee couplings are made before painting is started.

18 The wagons are completed with small details such as chain loops attached to the solebar; buffers and coupling hooks together with brake wheels fitted to the BR 'Salmon'. Some filling was needed to improve the appearance of both models.

19 The tension lock coupling brackets are not required when Kadee couplings are being used. They are cut off the bogie frames before painting.

20 Before starting painting there is one masking job to do to the models and that is to protect the bearings.

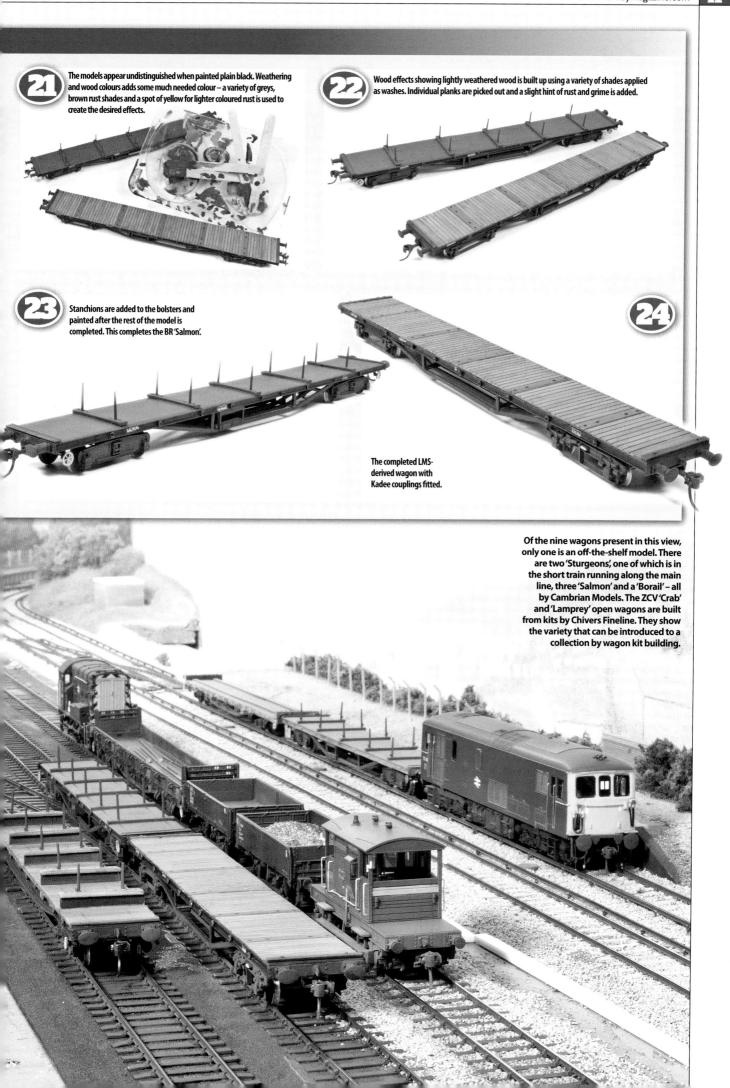

21 The models appear undistinguished when painted plain black. Weathering and wood colours adds some much needed colour – a variety of greys, brown rust shades and a spot of yellow for lighter coloured rust is used to create the desired effects.

22 Wood effects showing lightly weathered wood is built up using a variety of shades applied as washes. Individual planks are picked out and a slight hint of rust and grime is added.

23 Stanchions are added to the bolsters and painted after the rest of the model is completed. This completes the BR 'Salmon'.

24

The completed LMS-derived wagon with Kadee couplings fitted.

Of the nine wagons present in this view, only one is an off-the-shelf model. There are two 'Sturgeons', one of which is in the short train running along the main line, three 'Salmon' and a 'Borail' – all by Cambrian Models. The ZCV 'Crab' and 'Lamprey' open wagons are built from kits by Chivers Fineline. They show the variety that can be introduced to a collection by wagon kit building.

Landscaping with POLYST

HOW TO GUIDES

HERE AT *HORNBY MAGAZINE* we are always looking for quick, convenient and simple ways to build layouts. With every project we have a deadline to meet and that has meant developing methods that achieve results fast.

Shortley Bridge and Felton Cement Works uses our tried and tested method of creating the landscape of rolling hills and valleys – polystyrene blocks carved to shape and covered with plaster bandage.

This method has been used in hundreds of layouts and the beauty of it is how easily the landscape can be formed in a realistic manner simply by gluing blocks of polystyrene together. Its light weight also makes it ideal for exhibition layouts.

When it comes to the material there are lots of choices including specific model railway related products from Woodland Scenics collecting materials from packaging or, as shown in this feature, using readily available insulation sheet materials from DIY stores.

A landscape like the one shown here uses a lot of material. In total we have used two 8ft x 4ft sheets of polystyrene and there is a considerable amount of wastage when it comes to the carving process which is well worth considering if you are working on a tight budget. If that is the case then another simple method for creating a landscape is to use cardboard strips woven together to create a lattice which can be overlaid with plaster bandage, as shown in HM89.

Having used the block method several times before we are now well versed in the process. We glue the layers together with 'No More Nails' type adhesive and allow it to set for at least 24 hours before beginning the carving process.

Carving takes a keen eye and a sharp saw and is best attempted in multiple sessions allowing you to keep considering the overall effect of what you are working on. The landscape for Shortley Bridge was carved out to suit over three separate evenings. Be prepared for a lot of mess too – polystyrene is a messy material once you start cutting and carving it!

Having completed the carving process a suitable surface is required to apply grass turfs and fibres for the final scenic effects. The best medium we have found for this is plaster bandage cut into lengths around 9in long, dipped in water and then laid over the polystyrene landscape. At least two layers are applied over the whole scene for strength.

The final part of the process is to paint the whole landscape with brown poster paint. This reduces the potential for white chips occurring should the layout get knocked or damaged in transit.

With all this done Shortley Bridge is now ready for the application of grass textures and turfs to really bring it to life. ∎

There are several ways to create a realistic landscape, but one which is highly effective and quick to work with is based on polystyrene blocks. **MIKE WILD** reveals his method for creating landscapes with this easily shaped material.

YRENE

An 'L1' 2-6-4T rounds the curve past the cement works through the newly completed landscape. The plaster bandage surface has been painted with brown poster paint and is now ready for the first layers of grass to be applied.

CREATING A HARD SHELL LANDSCAPE

To begin the process polystyrene blocks are cut to shape to fit the area and glued together with 'No More Nails' adhesive to achieve the correct height around the railway and structures such as bridges and viaducts.

A sharp double sided hand saw will make light work of polystyrene. Make sure you leave the blocks for at least 24 hours for the adhesive to set properly – otherwise you will find the blocks move during shaping.

The near side of this cutting is complete and ready for covering with plaster bandage, whereas the area to the rear is awaiting shaping. A lot of height can be gained using this method leading to dramatic scenic effects.

On the approach to the fiddle yard after the cement works the cutting will form part of the scenic break. It has been carved away to suggest it rises towards an overbridge beyond the scenic break.

CREATING A HARD SHELL LANDSCAPE

Moving forwards, the blocks between the running line and cement works yard have now been shaped too. Don't be afraid to step away during the carving process to evaluate how it is coming together – fresh eyes make all the difference to the end result.

The cutting in front of the cement works has deliberately been kept low to open up views of the works to viewers at exhibitions. A single layer of 50mm polystryrene was used for this and in places it has been carved away to nothing.

Using 50mm blocks means high cuttings can be built up quickly. This is the raw blockwork to form a cutting around the curve to the cement works prior to carving…

…After carving the cutting takes on a much more subtle effect which will look realistic after covering with plaster bandage.

To cover the blockwork with plaster bandage you will need to cut rolls into strips around 9in long – sometimes smaller depending on what you are working around – and dip them into water to activate the plaster.

11

A double layer of plaster bandage is a wise move – it takes more time, but means the finished landscape will be durable.

10

Once wetted the plaster bandage needs to be transferred to the layout instantly. Take care to cover track when carrying out this process – it's easy to drip water from the bandage while laying it on the landscape.

12

The landscape is now ready for painting with poster paint. Having reached this stage we decided to add a little extra polystyrene around the riverbed before applying plaster bandage below the viaduct.

WHAT WE USED		
MATERIAL	**SOURCE**	**WEBSITE**
Polystyrene insulation blocks	DIY stores	*www.google.co.uk*
'No More Nails' adhesive	DIY stores	*www.google.co.uk*
Plaster bandage	Hobbycraft	*www.hobbycraft.co.uk*
Poster paint	Hobbycraft	*www.hobbycraft.co.uk*

A Class 25 draws a rake of cement wagons out of the yard. The low lying landscape between the main line and the sidings helps to distinguish the two areas of the layout while the cutting side to the right leads the viewer's eye into the scenic area.

Digital semaphores

Using readily available equipment **MIKE WILD** shows how semaphore signals can be brought fully into the digital era in just six simple steps.

THE SEMAPHORE SIGNAL is synonymous with the steam era railway and while there are still some on the main line network today they are a rapidly vanishing breed. Until recently modellers have had no choice but to build their own signals and have a ready supply of skills and patience in order to make them fully operational - that is until Dapol released its ready built working semaphores.

In the past *Hornby Magazine*'s layouts have always featured static signals, but with the advent of Dapol's ready made and fully operational semaphore signals covering upper and lower quadrant arms,

Shortley Bridge and Felton Cement Works will, ultimately, be fully signalled. For now only the single arm signals at the station and alongside the cement works will be operational as we are waiting for the bracket signals to be released by Dapol.

The principles of installation are very simple with the Dapol signals – drill a 14mm hole through the baseboard, pass the wires and motor base through the hole, clamp it in position and then wire

it up as per the supplied wiring diagram. However, they have been designed primarily for use with analogue control. Fortunately DCC specialist Train-Tech has developed a solution in its SC3 semaphore signal decoder, which has been designed specifically to work with Dapol signals.

This accessory decoder is simple to fit and takes out all the potential headaches of converting Dapol's signals to DCC

WHAT WE USED		
PRODUCT	**MANUFACTURER**	**CAT NO.**
7x 0.2mm multi-core equipment wire	*www.rapidonline.com*	GW010435
BR semaphore signal	*www.dapol.co.uk*	4L-002-001
Semaphore signal decoder	*www.train-tech.com*	SC3

HOW TO GUIDES

operation. All you have to do is follow the instructions, connect the right wires to the right terminals, add a DCC power supply and it will all work. It takes but a matter of minutes to connect signals to the SC3 decoder and because of its one touch addressing it takes only a matter of moments to set them up for future use too. Better still, each module controls two signals independently.

The advent of ready made working signals has been a long time coming, but Dapol has answered modellers' requests and is continuing to develop the range further. We can't wait to see the forthcoming bracket signals and start testing them on Shortley Bridge in the future. ∎

INSTALLING DCC POWERED SEMAPHORE SIGNALS

1  Working signals are a great addition to any model railway and these BR style semaphore signals from Dapol make a great feature. They are factory fitted with a motor and lamp behind the spectacle plate and are straightforward to fit.

2

First drill a 14mm diameter hole through the baseboard where you wish to install the signal using a large diameter wood drill bit.

3  We trimmed the base of the signal before installation to reduce its footprint, using a craft knife to carefully trim the plastic rectangle to size. The circular motor enclosure is then carefully passed through the baseboard ensuring the wires are inserted first.

4  Once pushed through the baseboard, fit the supplied plastic nut onto the circular base and tighten it up – not too tight though as this will impair movement of the mechanism. The wires are then connected to a specially designed Train Tech Dapol semaphore signal accessory decoder (Cat No. SC3) as detailed in the instruction sheet.

5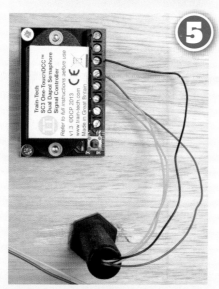

The Train Tech SC3 semaphore signal decoder has been specially designed to work with the Dapol signals and is pre-wired to suit. Connections are provided to allow two signals to be connected to each decoder.

6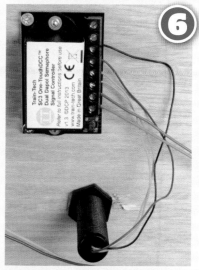

A power supply is then added to the signal decoder and connected back to the main power connection with the point motor feed. Once installed the Dapol semaphore signal is a neat finishing touch to the platform end and another working component of the layout.

THE VIADUCT SCENE

Viaducts and bridges can make spectacular scenic features, particularly when they cross water. **MIKE WILD** explains how to create a river scene using the Wills viaduct kit and readily available scenic products.

A BR Sulzer Type 2 crosses the newly installed viaduct with a mixed goods.

WATER TRICKLES PAST, lapping at the stones around the river edges, a swan and her cygnet paddling easily under a pretty three arch viaduct. In the distance the distinctive sound of a Sulzer engine working up the gradient echoes, gradually getting louder as it approaches. Suddenly it's above, vibrating the ground as the Type 2 works hard at the head of a mixed goods.

It's a scene we'd all love to savour and one that can be recreated in model form using readily available materials, a few hours of time and a bit of patience while the materials dry in between layers.

This viaduct scene uses the Wills three arch viaduct as its centrepiece. The kit has been cleverly designed to suit both double and single track formations simply by trimming the inner arch brick sheets down a pre-scribed line.

Assembly requires a sharp craft knife, a flat file or sanding board and liquid plastic cement. The components are cleanly moulded which makes assembly that much simpler and after cleaning up each can be joined together.

For this project we assembled the bridge around the trackbed. This has advantages and disadvantages. To assemble the bridge off the layout we would have painted and fully finished it before installing it. This would have slowed down the build time and also opened up potential for damaging the paint finish. However, building the bridge on the layout means that it can be fixed in position early on and progress with the overall scene can move forward quickly – the only downside is that painting of the stonework is more awkward.

Any river scene needs water to look the part and for this project we used Woodland Scenics realistic water. This purpose-made material dries clear and creates a superb water effect. However,

like all real water it runs when poured so each end of the riverbed has to be capped to stop it running off the edge of the baseboard while drying. To do this we used baking parchment or greaseproof paper clamped to the baseboard edges using a block of wood. This holds the water in while it cures, and it peels away without making any marks or pulling on the cured water when it's all done.

The finished look of a river scene isn't down to any individual component but how they are combined together. If you are planning to build such a scene, take your time, step back every now and then and take pictures of your work. It will help show up areas which need more attention and where you need to do no more.

The step by step guide explains the steps we went through to develop the viaduct scene for Shortley Bridge. ∎

WHAT WE USED		
PRODUCT	**MANUFACTURER**	**CAT NO.**
Plaster bandage	Various sources	Various
Fine blended green turf	Woodland Scenics	WT1349
Fine leaf foliage, light green	Woodland Scenics	WF1132
Fine leaf foliage, olive green	Woodland Scenics	WF1133
Realistic water	Woodland Scenics	WC1211
Extra coarse talus rocks	Woodland Scenics	WC1273
Fine blended grey ballast	Woodland Scenics	WB1393
Coarse blended grey ballast	Woodland Scenics	WB1395
Autumn 6.5mm static grass	MiniNatur	006-33
Winter 6.5mm static grass	MiniNatur	006-34
Autumn 4.5mm static grass	MiniNatur	004-23
Winter 4.5mm static grass	MiniNatur	006-24
Swans and cygnets	Langley Models	F123p
Lime mortar	Lifecolor	UA742
Dark stone, matt	Humbrol	187

With a heavily laden cement working, a 'WD' 2-8-0 slogs across the viaduct heading for Shortley Bridge.

BUILDING A VIADUCT AND RIVER SCENE

1 The starting point is assembly of the viaduct. The model used here is the Wills kit for a three arch viaduct which can be extended with additional arches. We reduced its width from double to single track and assembled it around the 9mm thick plywood base.

2 Assembling the viaduct on the layout has more advantages than disadvantages – the only downside being that painting is slightly awkward. However, it does mean that we can save the painting until the very end so that any spills or splashes of other colours and turfs won't affect its final appearance.

3 The landscape is built up in blocks using polystyrene as shown in the landscaping feature on pages 44-47. This method is quick and simple and allows rolling hills to be developed.

4 The polystyrene is carved away to create the riverbed. The lower sections were added to after this image to finalise the position of the river.

BUILDING A VIADUCT AND RIVER SCENE

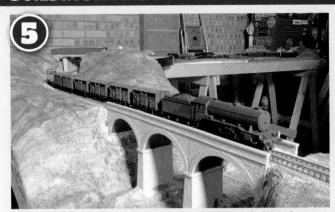

The whole riverbed was then covered with plaster bandage as described in the landscaping feature.

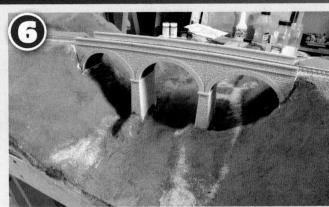

Next the ground was covered with Woodland Scenics fine blended green turf with Woodland Scenics fine blended grey ballast used around the edges to create pathways. Neat PVA glue spread with a damp brush holds this base layer in place.

With the first layer of static grass applied the scenery around the river begins to gain depth. The static grass is fixed in place with diluted PVA glue which has been applied carefully to the base layer of grass with a brush to avoid contact with the ballasted areas.

A second layer of static grass fixed with 50:50 diluted PVA and water increases the depth of the grass. A happy accident meant the glue ran into the riverbed and an attempt to clear away the excess grass with a brush created what we felt was the effect of weeds on the riverbed.

As a final addition before pouring the water, Woodland Scenics talus, light grey rocks and various ballasts were used to create piles of rocks around the river edges and in it too. The larger talus rocks were placed first followed by finer grades to set them in position. All are loose at this stage.

For the water effects we are using Woodland Scenics realistic water – a liquid which will soon run off the baseboard edge if uncontained. To hold the water in place we clamped a strip of baking parchment using a block of wood at each end of the riverbed. This greaseproof paper won't adhere to the realistic water, making it easy to remove once the water has cured.

The realistic water can then be poured into the riverbed. Build it up in thin layers as the first will help seal the riverbed. In total we made four applications using two bottles of realistic water for the final effect.

With the messy work of plaster bandage, brown paint, grasses and water complete we moved on to paint the viaduct. The stonework was first painted with a solid coat of Lifecolor lime mortar (UA742) as a base for further work.

The stonework was then dry brushed with Humbrol dark stone No 187 with the arch stones picked out in the same colour. The brick lining inside the arches was dry brushed with the same colour to tone down its appearance.

Building up the detail, Woodland Scenics fine leaf foliage was planted around the viaduct to bed the structure into its surrounding. This material isn't cheap, but it is superb for bedding in structures quickly and effectively.

Additional grass textures were added to the riverbanks by spraying them carefully with extra hold hairspray and dusting Woodland Scenics fine blended green turf and other flocks. See feature on pages 86-91 for more on grass textures.

Not wanting to go over the top, we added one final detail to the scene – two swans and cygnets coming through the narrow channel around the left-band pier. These are from Langley Models' pre-painted selection.

Country branch
TRAIN

Using off-the-shelf weathering products, **TIM SHACKLETON** goes back in time to recreate a typical cross-country train of the late 1950s…

WEATHERING a three-coach passenger train for *Hornby Magazine's* Shortley Bridge layout was an opportunity to integrate locomotive and rolling stock into a coherent whole. It also allowed me bring out some subtle (and not so subtle) variations and explore the properties of different weathering techniques.

The individual models I was working on were – with one exception – all characteristic of the chosen area at that particular era. These days, of course, it's easy to get hold of the appropriate locomotives and coaches for the place and period you're modelling – the big challenge lies in showing them in typical condition for the time. There was nothing 'chocolate box', I can assure you, about the steam trains winding their way through the British countryside in the pre-Beeching era. They were slow and dirty,

not especially comfortable and only the railway enthusiast would have found the journey a pleasurable one. That was the sense I was trying to evoke here.

The subject of choice is a pair of Thompson 'L1' 2-6-4Ts using the fabulous and detailed Hornby model as the basis. Throughout their brief lives, the 'L1s' had an extremely limited sphere of operation – outer suburban duties on Eastern Region lines out of London (Liverpool Street, King's Cross and Marylebone), a few out to grass in Norfolk and Suffolk, and a handful on ex-North Eastern lines around Darlington. Woodford Halse had the odd one and occasionally sent them out as far as Banbury. Others were at Gorton shed for the ex Great Central lines in the Manchester area and in the final years of the class, a fair number congregated at Colwick for use on local trains in the Nottingham district (Derby and Grantham were the usual destinations).

Towards the end a handful strayed, for no

obvious reason, into the West Riding of Yorkshire but they were not popular and their use was limited.

My brief was to prepare two 'L1s' for the *Hornby Magazine* project – it was my choice to make them as different as humanly possible. I always like to ring the changes and include a little subtle variety but this time there was a snag. Hornby's model of Robert Stephenson & Hawthorn-built 67777 was no problem as this was a local engine throughout its life. However, modelling 67722 which is one of the engines from the original Darlington batch - 67700-67730 - which had a number of significant differences – could have been difficult. Being Westinghouse-fitted, these engines were normally found only in Great Eastern territory but, since they came back to North Road every few years for heavy repairs, they could be seen on running-in turns in the area before being sent home. That solved the problem rather neatly, I thought. ∎

WEATHERING A PAIR OF THOMPSON 'L1' 2-6-4TS

1

With the 'L1' Hornby has excelled on points of detail and differences between batches. Most of the interest focuses on the right-hand side of the locomotive. 67722 represents one of the early Darlington-built engines with Westinghouse brake pump and riveted cab roof. 67777 is a later engine with part welded roof, cutaway front platform and solid front steps. Interestingly, 67722 has the full height cab door with which these engines were fitted between 1955 and 1960.

2

Before fitting the detail parts, I've given 67722 an airbrushed coat of Johnson's Klear floor polish to replicate the ex-works finish I wanted to achieve. It's fast drying and pretty tough, but I left it for 24 hours before doing anything else. The paintwork immediately acquires the lustrous blackberry black of a freshly outshopped engine.

3

Meanwhile, I've airbrushed a light application of road dirt/brake block dust over the lower part of 67777. For years I've mixed up a combination of matt black and Humbrol 'Matt Leather' (62) to achieve the desired shade but of late the latter colour seems to have taken on a distinct green tinge that I don't like. A hefty slug of orange in the form of Revell No 85 (which the manufacturer calls 'Brown') seems to restore the balance.

4

The boiler and upper works of 67777 are airbrushed with enamel paints from the same palette but with much more black in the mix. On a grubby locomotive the red lining on the boiler bands would quickly disappear under a coat of soot, cinders and other assorted nasties. I've also sprayed some of the same mix over the wheels, frame and motion to give a subtly varied discoloration.

Work-weary RSH-built 67777 approaching from the left is a Darlington-allocated engine that spent its whole life in the area. It has the large 10in numbers sometimes seen on engines overhauled at North Road works and it also has the low (and very draughty) cab doors that were often the subject of complaints. Fresh from overhaul at Darlingon works, 67722 in the foreground will shortly be returning to its home shed, Bishop's Stortford, complete with a fresh coat of paint, the new post-1956 emblem and replacement full-height 'limousine' cab doors. The brightwork has been polished and the engine gleams like a new pin.

WEATHERING A PAIR OF THOMPSON 'L1' 2-6-4TS

⑤ Enamel paints have a generous drying time which allows us to partially 'clean' the model using a flat brush. Take the paint off with gentle downward strokes, allowing it to collect in corners just as it does on the prototype. Real locomotive weathering has a random, patchy, uneven look – it doesn't look like it's been applied by airbrush!

⑥ Having taken off as much paint as I want, I've put a gentle waft of Revell 'Anthracite' (No 9) over the tanks and bunker sides, giving the impression of the inexorable accumulation of dirt over time. Weathering needs to give the impression of layers building up on top of what is already there.

⑦

⑧

As soon as a locomotive is in steam, dirt begins to accumulate – even while it is standing on shed. Usually the first signs of life are soot building up on the cab roof, and the smokebox starting to discolour to a warm metallic shade. For ex works 67722 I used 'Burned Black' (UA736) from LifeColor's useful 'Black Rubber' set. I used more of the same shade on the wheels. Only the very gentlest misting is needed.

Running plates and the front platform quickly discolour – this I represented with a light dusting of MIG 'Rubble Dust' powder (P234) applied with a small, square-tipped nylon brush.

⑨ More powders on the cab roof and smokebox, to give a little tonal variety. Here I've used MIG 'Black Smoke' (P023) and a touch of 'Old Grease' (GP11) from the Adam Wilder 'Gunpowder' range.

⑩ Steam locomotives use a lot of oil and the working parts are usually swimming in the stuff. On the Westinghouse pump and mechanical lubricators I used AK Interactive's 'Engine Oil' (084) applied by brush.

67722 was built in 1948 and spent its working life on services to and from Liverpool Street, for which it carried Westinghouse brake equipment. It has the curved front platform fitted to the first batch of Darlington-built engines, as well as the full-height cab doors fitted from 1955 on. Minor repairs would have been carried out at Stratford or Doncaster but for overhauls it would return to Darlington.

11

The motion of locomotives in works would often be cleaned and scoured back to bare metal before being coated in a protective grease. This had a distinctly tan colour which I represent with Revell No 80 'Mud Brown' (Humbrol No 9 'Tan' is much the same). AK's 'Engine Oil' is good in this context, as is Wilder 'Diesel Effect' (NL31).

12

Using a variety of oily colours gives a prototypical range, from light brown through to almost black. Motion didn't last long in this state but it was a distinctive feature of ex-works locomotives like 67722.

13

The 9v battery enables me to turn the wheels over under power and reach the front coupling rods where they've been hidden by the motion. This avoids the telltale shadows you'd otherwise get on the wheels.

14

Going back to the grubby 'L1', I put some very subtle discoloration and rainwater streaks on the boiler by using a stiff, nylon-bristled brush to apply tiny dabs of AK Interactive's 'European Earth' powder (AK042). Work it well in.

WEATHERING A PAIR OF THOMPSON 'L1' 2-6-4TS

More AK weathering powders are used to represent the build-up of rust around areas where water would accumulate and cause corrosion. Rust isn't just one shade, but several – here I used three different tones.

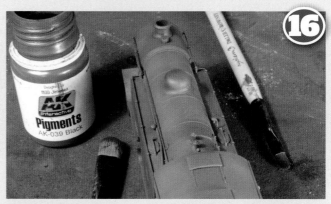

You can mix weathering powders just as you would with paints. Here I've toned down the brightness of the rust on the tank tops and smokebox using AK Interactive's black pigment (AK039).

WHAT WE USED

PRODUCT	MANUFACTURER	CAT NO.
Black pigment	AK Interactive	AK039
European earth	AK Interactive	AK042
Engine oil	AK Interactive	AK084
Old grease	Wilder	GP11
Diesel effect	Wilder	NL31
Frame dirt	Lifecolor	UA719
Track dirt	Lifecolor	UA720
Roof dirt	Lifecolor	UA722
Weathered black	Lifecolor	UA723
Brake dust	Lifecolor	UA724
Burned black	Lifecolor	UA736
Matt black	Humbrol	33
Matt leather	Humbrol	62
Black smoke	MIG	P023
Light rust	MIG	P024
Dark wash	MIG	P220
Rubble dust	MIG	P234
Anthracite	Revell	9
Mud brown	Revell	80
Orange	Revell	85

USEFUL LINKS

- **AK Interactive** *www.ak-interactive.com*
- **Lifecolor** *www.airbrushes.com*
- **Wilder** *www.airbrushes.com*
- **Humbrol** *www.humbrol.co.uk*
- **Mig Productions** *www.migproductions.com*
- **Revell** *www.revell.com*

Cylinder fronts turn a distinctive orange shade that can be overpowering if you're heavy handed. MIG 'Light Rust' (P024) captures the colour perfectly.

Seen side by side, the two locomotives present quite a contrast. 67777 in the foreground is in typical condition for a locomotive of the 1950s and early 1960s – grubby and unkempt, but far from totally disreputable. 67722 behind shows what an engine would look a few days after being released from the paint shop. For every locomotive in this kind of condition, you saw hundreds that looked more like 67777.

E 82798 E

67777

THE COACHING STOCK

I saw very few 'L1s' but when it came to weathering the coaches – examples of Hornby's popular Thompson non-corridor stock – I had a lot of memories to draw on. This is important because, while interest in modelling the railways of 50 and 60 years ago continues to grow, there are fewer and fewer people around with direct first-hand experience of what train travel was like in the pre-Beeching era.

My overwhelming recollection is of an all-pervasive dinginess on main-line services as well as stopping trains. Coach sides were usually clean enough – though oily dirt congregated around door hinges and window ventilators – but the roofs and underframes were universally filthy. The motion was anything but smooth – a lurching, backwards and forwards surge punctuated by the clatter of rail joints. Interiors were drab, dusty and uncomfortable, while windows were often smeary and hard to see through clearly.

In winter carriages were either unbearably stuffy or unheated. There was a permanent whiff of stale tobacco – only a small portion of the accommodation was non-smoking – while drifting smoke and steam added a distinctive

tinge to the aroma of 1950s travel. First Class – which no one ever travelled in on the trains I was on – had a Sunday-parlour feel to it, unwelcoming and a bit chill.

Journeys on steam specials and on preserved lines bear very little resemblance to the real thing, even though you're probably travelling in the same kind of vehicle. It all seems a bit sanitised to me, so I thought it would be interesting to recreate this typical stopping passenger train of the late 1950s exactly as I remember them, and using period photographs as my reference point.

Everything you need for weathering your coaches is in this image – an airbrush (in this instance a trigger-action Iwata Neo TRN-2), a set of LifeColor's 'Rail Weathering' acrylic paints and some MIG enamel 'Dark Wash' (P220).

Using a good-quality fine brush (Size 0 is perfect) dipped in the dark wash, touch in the door openings, droplight windows and door stops. The paint will simply flash along the lines, emphasising detail, creating false shadows and suggesting dirt build-up. If you get any on the coach side, wipe it off with a tissue dipped in white spirit.

The coach wheels need to be painted separately using an old brush – the bristles will get caught on the details so there's no point wasting a good one on this kind of work. The coach is inverted in a foam cradle. The paint mix is predominantly 'Frame Dirt' (UA 719) to which I've added some 'Brake Dust' (UA 724) and a touch of 'Track Dirt' (UA 720).

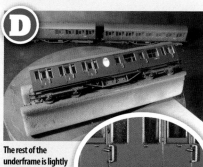

Using the same masking technique with the piece of card, I've airbrushed the coach roofs using 'Roof Dirt' (UA 722). For a little tonal variety I've drifted some 'Weathered Black' (UA 723) over the middle coach roof. Like most good weathering, the differences are subtle but this is the kind of touch that really brings a model to life.

The rest of the underframe is lightly airbrushed with a similar paint mix. To avoid getting paint on the sides – which are to remain clean – I use a simple card mask held against the coach body. Masking tape does the same job. Tipping the coach back in the foam cradle enables me to reach the underframe details below the floor.

A nice detail touch is to represent the build-up of oily deposits around the axleboxes using 'Weathered Black'. With a quality airbrush like the Iwata you can spray from very close in – a centimetre or less.

The outward appearance of locomotives varied enormously but coaching stock – being cleaned reasonably regularly – tended to be a bit more consistent. The same is as true today as it was 50 years ago.

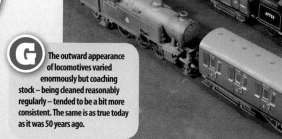

67777 was built by Robert Stephenson & Hawthorn of Newcastle and entered service in January 1950. It has a cutaway front platform and the original cab openings. It rarely strayed far from the Darlington area of the North Eastern Region but in its last months was transferred to Ardsley for trip freight duties. The 'L1s' were not popular in the West Riding and did little useful work before they were withdrawn en masse in 1962.

MASTER
in the Gallery

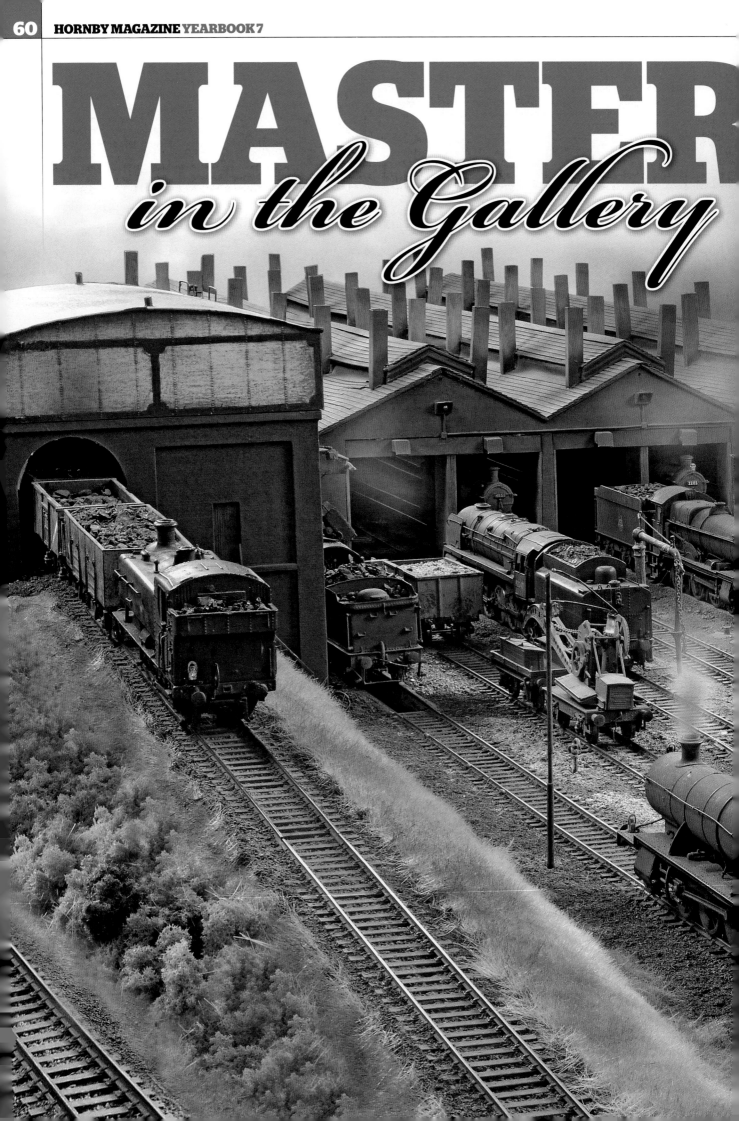

PIECES

In this special feature we highlight some of the very best layouts and photographs to have been featured in *Hornby Magazine* over the past year. Prepare to be inspired…

Kensal Green – Built to represent a London area Western Region motive power depot, Kensal Green is now enjoying a second lease of life having transferred from its original owners to Graham Tavener. It has been overhauled and brought into the digital age and is once again back on the exhibition circuit. Kensal Green featured in HM82.
Trevor Jones/Hornby Magazine.

Broxfield – BR's Eastern Region around London is the inspiration for Broxfield – an intensively operated four-track main line scene with everything a model railway builder could want. Builder Roger Lattimore wanted to recapture his childhood memories in 'OO' gauge and this layout continues to develop. Broxfield featured in **HM81.** *Trevor Jones/Hornby Magazine.*

Dubmill Sidings – This 40ft long 'O' gauge freight yard is Steve Thompson's latest creation which models a busy scene in the final years of the 1960s, just after the end of steam and just before the introduction of the TOPS numbering scheme. In this scene a 'Deltic' draws into the yard with the daily parcels working as a Class 20 heads out on the branch with a rake of steel flats for loading. Dubmill Sidings featured in **HM78.** *Mike Wild/Hornby Magazine.*

Knight's Hill – The sun has set over North Cornwall and the residents of Knight's Hill have the lights turned on. Business on the railway continues in this might-have-been early preservation scene produced by Malcolm Briggs. Knight's Hill featured in HM86.
Trevor Jones/*Hornby Magazine*.

Whitby West Cliff – Brad Seaman set out to produce a model of Whitby West Cliff and Upgang viaduct in 'OO' scale and so far it totals 40ft in length with further sections under construction to extend it even further. This is Upgang viaduct, built entirely from scratch with plastic section, being crossed by a 'G5' 0-4-4T piloting a 'B1' 4-6-0. Whitby West Cliff featured in **HM85.** *Mike Wild/Hornby Magazine.*

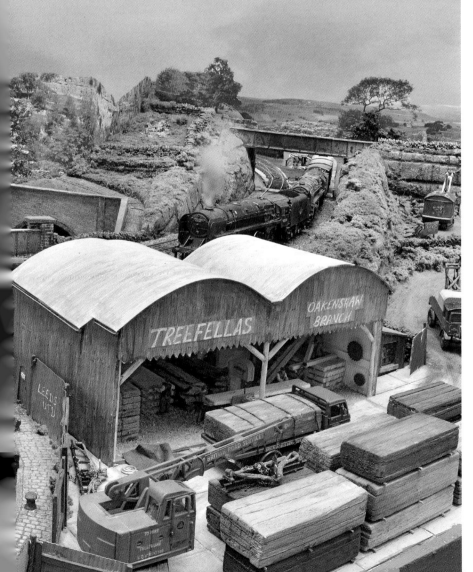

Above left: **Leicester South GC – The Shipley Model Railway Society** is the proud owner of this model of Leicester South on the Great Central Main Line as it was in the mid-1950s. A BR lined blue Gresley 'A3' 4-6-2 thunders past the goods yard with the 'Master Cutler' recreating a scene from more than 50 years ago. Leicester South GC featured in HM79. Derek Shore/*Hornby Magazine*.

Above: **Great Wakering garden railway** – Hornby Magazine photographer and model maker Trevor Jones' stunning 'OO' gauge garden railway continues to develop and amongst his most recent projects is the rebuilding of this tunnel into a new scene. A BR 'Britannia' 4-6-2 passes the site of excavations with an express. Great Wakering featured in HM85's Garden Railway supplement. Trevor Jones/*Hornby Magazine*.

Left: **Oakenshaw – The Redditch Model Railway Club's** latest layout is this superb model of a West Yorkshire town set in the 1950s and early 1960s period. Oakenshaw features entirely scratch built buildings and structures together with a superb atmosphere. Heavy freights pass through above the timber yard on the approach to the station. Oakenshaw featured in HM88. Trevor Jones/*Hornby Magazine*.

Above left: **Foxdale Depot – Capturing the spirit of an industrial railway in the late 1940s, Mick Payne's Foxdale Depot is a fascinating take on railway operations. An Andrew Barclay 0-4-0ST runs through the yard as a coal merchant's lorry approaches the crossing. Foxdale Depot featured in HM83.** Trevor Jones/*Hornby Magazine.*

Above: **Woodmores Scrapyard – Two staff are employed break up a BR 'Standard Four' 2-6-0 in Woodmores Scrapyard, a reminder of the end for many hard working steam locomotives. Built to 4mm scale by Michael Russell this stunning scrapyard scene took inspiration from the famous yard of Woodhams in Barry South Wales. Woodmores Scrapyard featured in HM81.** Michael Russell.

Left: **Woodhead – The Woodhead route through the Pennine hills has long been a source of intrigue and passion for railway modellers and Gary Atkinson recreated the tunnel and its approaches in 'N' gauge. Double headed Class 76 electrics pass at Woodhead station recreating a scene from the early 1970s. Woodhead featured in HM87.** Mike Wild/*Hornby Magazine.*

Belmont Road – The night air is filled with the sound of steam at Belmont Road depot as locomotives are kept warm through the night ready for their next duties. Owned by Colin Snowdon this superbly atmospheric depot occupies a single 4ft x 2ft 6in baseboard, but has all the facilities you could want for steam depot. Belmont Road featured in HM86. *Trevor Jones/Hornby Magazine.*

Two Type 2s

PAUL CHETTER demonstrates alternative ways to overcome design obstacles, both model and prototype, to install DCC sound into a Bachmann Class 25 and a Heljan Class 27.

The Bachmann Class 25 (left) and Heljan Class 27 (right) demand different approaches to speaker installation for DCC sound. Once finished the internal changes are invisible on the outside.

ALTHOUGH DIGITAL Command Control (DCC) sound has been available for UK locomotives for several years now, there are still a large number of models based on designs originating in the non-sound fitted past. Inevitably, no thought had been given to provision of suitable speaker location or enclosures at that time.

In such cases, those who wish to add sound have to incorporate ad hoc arrangements to house the speaker and, occasionally, the decoder too. An ingenious assortment of individual methods has evolved, sometimes aided by new products, like the 'sugar cube' speakers, which are now widely available.

Recently, some aftermarket products have become available which have been designed to provide a reliable and consistent way to fit speakers to a limited range of models and we will explore some of these later.

Of course, differences in the design or equipment fitted to real locomotives can sometimes cause a corresponding reduction of available free space in the model. With diesel locomotive models, the fuel tanks, battery boxes and equipment boxes are often stowed below the engine room floor. In many models, these may provide the largest uncluttered space available, and have become the first place to consider as the speaker housing.

At the same time, there is a common belief that this position, with the speaker facing downwards towards the track, provides the best audio experience too.

I know from my own testing and past experience that this is not always the case and many other factors play a part in optimal performance. Often, the reality is that a compromise between ease of installation and sound quality has to be reached.

It's against this background that these particular models, of notionally very similar prototypes, were selected to illustrate ways in which to install a speaker.

Each was designed to accommodate a decoder and that aspect is entirely straightforward, though the lack of 8-pin socket orientation markings in the Heljan model is mildly awkward. I used a Zimo MX644D 21-pin decoder in the Bachmann Class 25 whilst the Heljan Class 27 was fitted with an 8-pin MX645R. I created and loaded a custom sound project for each locomotive type, now available from Digitrains.

Bachmann Class 25

This model is a representation of a locomotive built for freight duties. No steam boiler or water tanks for train heating were required and so repositioning of other equipment left the fuel tank as the largest storage component below the floor.

It might be possible to utilise this space, but it is restrictively small covering half the length between the bogies. A 23mm round, or a pair of 'cube' speakers could be used. On the other hand, access would require removal of the bogies and de-soldering of connections to the model's Printed Circuit Board (PCB), and a custom housing would need to be constructed.

Whilst this is not beyond many modellers' capabilities, I decided to use a simple method to create a 'tortured path' installation that I have previously used to good effect. This required the removal of the dummy fan and carving away its shroud from the inside of the model to allow a 20mm x 40 mm speaker to be sealed, facing upwards under the grille, to the roof with glue, mastic or silicon sealer. The fan can be trimmed and re-fixed under the grille if required, but I left it out to allow the greatest possible area for the sound to escape. The fan would be barely visible, so little is lost from the external appearance.

Connection of two wires to the speaker and the marked positions on the PCB, and minor adjustment to the power supply arrangement for the headcode lighting finished the work required, prior to final reassembly.

WHAT WE USED		
PRORDUCT	**SUPPLIER**	**PRICE**
Bachmann Class 25	*www.bachmann.com*	£94.95
Heljan Class 27	*www.heljan.dk*	£99.95
Zimo MX645R Sound Decoder	*www.digitrains.co.uk*	£85.00
Zimo MX644D Sound Decoder	*www.digitrains.co.uk*	£83.00
ABS 28 x 40mm speaker 2W	*www.digitrains.co.uk*	£5.50
28 x 40mm Class 27 cast enclosure plus speaker 3W	*www.dckits-devideos.co.uk*	£15.00
20 x 40mm Class 27 3D printed enclosure plus speaker	*www.dckits-devideos.co.uk*	£20.00
SC68 'stay alive' capacitor	*www.railexclusive.com*	£22.00

to the fore...

Heljan Class 27

The internal design of the Heljan model makes no concession towards sound fitting. It is feasible to fit a small round speaker under the roof grille, angled to clear the PCB, but unless you are willing to undertake serious reworking of the PCB and the subsequent re-wiring necessary, it is not possible to fit a 20mm x 40mm speaker in the same way as the Class 25. Fortunately, due to the model's construction and the real locomotives' original equipment, there is plenty of free space in the under-floor mouldings.

In HM83 I showed how to create speaker enclosures by modifying the existing mouldings on Heljan Class 33 models. For the Class 27 I decided to try the options offered by DC Kits – see panel on page 75.

Fitting the decoder was easy enough and I twisted the wiring harness to take up the slack. A blob of mastic or some double-sided tape will hold the decoder in place. The most difficult aspect was how to get the speaker wires from the decoder to the underside of the chassis. For me, the usual way is to carefully drill a pathway from the chassis bottom to its 'shoulder', making sure

that the wires will not pass across any windows when the body is replaced. With the speaker wires threaded through to the underside, all the subsequent work is done externally, so the body can be refitted.

The resin cast enclosure is a complete replacement for the Heljan components and the simplest to use. A hole must be drilled in the appropriate position for the speaker wires to pass through prior to connection to the speaker, which in turn is clipped into place. The whole unit was then fitted into the correct position and held with mastic, though a spot or two of your favourite glue would make a more secure attachment.

The time saving gained and the reassurance given by such a simple method giving consistent results will commend this alternative to many modellers. Some minor gap filling and aesthetic fettling around the speaker may be desired, though this surface will not be seen in service. What is noticeable on close inspection is that the casting is slightly deeper than the original, presumably to accommodate the considerable extra bulk of the 28mm x 40mm speaker with its large magnet as supplied.

I then repeated the exercise using the 3D printed version, and a 20mm x 40mm speaker. The attention to detail at the design stage makes this almost as easy to use despite the additional work required. The re-use of the Heljan parts ensures that there is virtually no visible difference from the standard model. Each version has its merits and it comes down to personal choice as to which you might use.

The elegance of the design and the final overall look when fitted makes the 3D printed enclosure the more accurate visually. The 20mm x 40mm speaker is available in 4, 8 or 100ohms varieties, so an exact match to your decoder's requirements is possible.

The slightly bulkier outline of the cast resin version means it loses out in the beauty stakes, but the speaker it houses is a real powerhouse, at 4ohms and 3W it is perfectly matched with the Zimo decoder driving it. This package is also the least expensive option of the two.

Then, just as we were about to go to press, Zimo launched a mid-range 'stay alive' capacitor which I was keen to use in the Class 27. At 6,800μF it will provide enough stored energy to turn the wheels by about ¼ of a revolution, enough for most circumstances. The package is a flat oblong shape which fits easily within the roof space of this model, and is specifically recommended for use with the MX645 decoder.

The Step by Step guides following show exactly how we went about installing these decoders and speakers into this pair of highly usable BR Type 2s. ■

SPEAKER OPTIMISATION

● Speakers work best when the sound emitted from the front is separated from sound emitted from the rear. A common way to achieve this in models is to totally enclose the back of the speaker - airtight but incorporating sufficient air to avoid the dampening effects of back pressure. Other ways include using a 'tuned' ported enclosure or creation of a 'tortured path' for the rear waves to escape in a controlled fashion that avoids interfering with the frontal sound waves. For more on this see HM85.

INSTALLING DCC SOUND IN A BACHMANN CLASS 25

1 The sparse underframe of the real locomotive means that the model has restricted space available below the solebar for speaker accommodation.

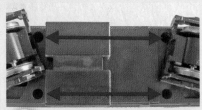

2 After releasing the four retaining screws inside these recesses (arrowed), the body can be lifted from the chassis.

3 To gain access to the fan shroud, release two screws and remove the fan assembly.

4 Similarly, remove the headcode illumination box, noting the two metal contacts.

5 When fitted, the speaker will be very close to these contacts. I bent them gently until they were straighter and at a steeper angle.

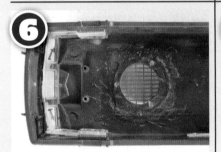

6 I carved away the shroud to allow the speaker to fit flush to the underside of the roof, below the fan grille. I also trimmed the fan to fit under the grille, but finally decided to leave it out to obtain the largest area from which the sounds could escape.

7 A 'dry run' with speaker and headcode illumination in place proved my calculations were correct and the installation could proceed.

8 Cheap and cheerful yet very effective. Using sticky mastic, the speaker was sealed to the roof which then became the baffle plate. Pay careful attention to fully sealing the two ends.

9 Insulation tape placed over the speaker frame will prevent shorting. The decoder's Function Outputs are internally protected to some extent, but there's no point in taking unnecessary risks.

10 On the chassis top there is a small PCB with exposed pads designed to make contact with the 'prongs' from the head code unit. This is now too high and would foul the speaker.

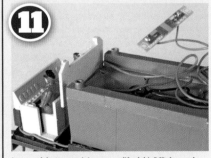

11 I removed the two retaining screws, lifted this PCB clear and reduced the height of the mounting turrets by about 50% using a small file. With the PCB reattached I checked that the illumination was working correctly.

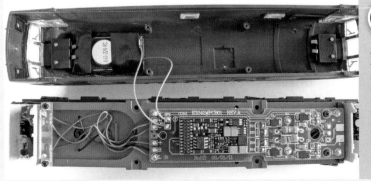

12 I soldered the speaker wires to the designated positions on the main PCB and added some insulation tape to protect the exposed speaker terminals. The decoder's amplifier is very vulnerable to damage if any shorting was to occur. The front and rear pads and the prongs which make contact with them when the body is refitted can be clearly seen. A visual trick of the perspective appears to show they would not meet, but in reality they line up quite nicely.

TIP

To gain the best performance from any DCC sound speaker, the rear needs to be enclosed fully to stop unwanted sounds interferring with those leaving the front of the speaker. This can be done in a number of ways including using mastik or bespoke enclosures.

Bespoke Sound Enclosures

In response to a lack of good speaker provision by model manufacturers a small number of solutions have been developed to provide simple, accurate assembly and fitting of appropriate speakers which even inexperienced modellers can use with confidence. To achieve this, these bespoke designs have been optimised for specific model and speaker combinations. The number of such solutions is limited at the moment, but more will undoubtedly become available as the popularity of DCC sound increases.

THE VITRAINS CLASS 47

The first publicly available solution was the kit sold by Rail Exclusive, which is still available. It was developed from a design I created for its limited edition ViTrains Class 47.

After much testing, a 'tortured path' solution was found to be optimal for that model. Using ViTrains production drawings to ensure accurate dimensions and inner roof profile, a laser-cut mounting frame was designed around a 28mm x 40mm speaker. I incorporated a stretcher bar to locate the re-used fans at the correct spacing and a gauging tab to ensure that when the whole assembly is fixed in place, the fans were automatically centralised within the roof grilles.

Finally, the assembly is fastened to the speaker to form a rigid unit. The close tolerances of the fit make it easy to obtain the airtight seal required when installed inside the model.

Currently, this solution is available only as a complete kit including a Zimo MX645R sound decoder, 28mm x 40mm speaker and the mounting kit.

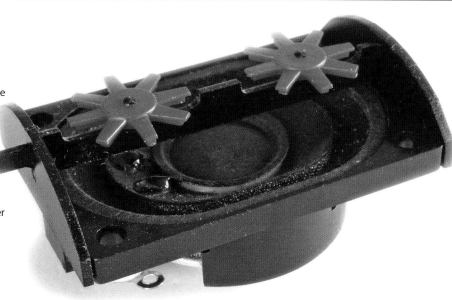

CAST RESIN

There are two Heljan models currently catered for by DC Kits' own design the Heljan Class 27 (as shown in the step by step guide) and the Class 33 as shown here.

Each is a one-piece cast resin enclosure which entirely replaces the underfloor mouldings, making them virtually 'plug and play'. Each is designed to accommodate a 28mm x 40mm speaker. They are available separately or complete with speaker.

I found them very easy to use giving a good sonic output. Unlike the other solutions here, they remain exposed to full view when fitted, so direct visual comparisons may seem a little unfair. However, the excellent, but bulky, speaker

requires the casting to be a couple of millimetres deeper than the Heljan originals.

3D PRINTED ENCLOSURE

DC Kits also markets an alternative solution for each of the same Heljan models and the Hornby Class 60. These are 3D printed enclosures designed by Ian Bishop. In essence, each is a box to which are added a 20mm x 40mm speaker and the outer parts of the Heljan mouldings in the case of the first two examples. But that understates the attention to detail Ian has paid to the initial design.

On the rear of the enclosure a hole feeds into a groove running the entire length for speaker wires to be fitted whilst allowing the base to fit flush to the model. The Heljan fixing tabs are replicated ensuring correct positioning and, although I found that I needed to trim the inside edges of these tabs a little, the design works well.

On the longer sides of the enclosure are holes which correspond to the pegs forming part of the outer components of the Heljan

mouldings. These are asymmetrically arranged, having clear left and right hand sides.

They are not glued together but a little care is required to separate the original unit into its component parts without damaging the fixing pegs. They can then be attached to the enclosure 'core' using the holes provided.

Equally well thought out, speaker fixing is a push-fit design. A bead along each long side holds it snugly whilst corner fillets serve to add support for the speaker and block off the unused mounting holes.

INSTALLING DCC SOUND IN A HELJAN CLASS 27

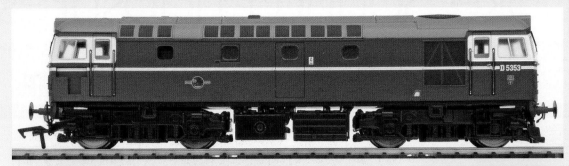

1 On the real locomotive from the appropriate angle, daylight can be seen above the battery boxes. This is featured on the model. Unfortunately, for optimum sound performance, this gap will have to be sealed.

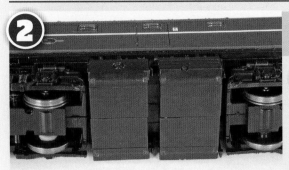

Similarly, we will need to enclose the air space between the boxes and fuel tanks.

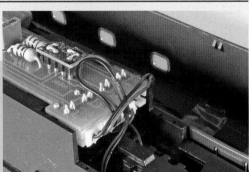

3 The body was released by gently prising the lower sides outwards to disengage the retaining lugs and lifting it upwards. This model uses plugged connections for power to the headcode illumination. Remove one from each end to free the body.

4 Although relatively uncluttered, the high shoulders of the chassis and the location of the DCC socket partially below the roof grille rules out fitting a 20mm x 40mm speaker. It is just possible to fit a small round speaker at an angle and sealed below the grille.

5 Having decided to use a speaker mounted below floor level, I used a pin-vice and a 2mm bit to drill a pathway for the speaker wires. I normally use this technique as it avoids possible snagging of wires if passed through the bogie spaces.

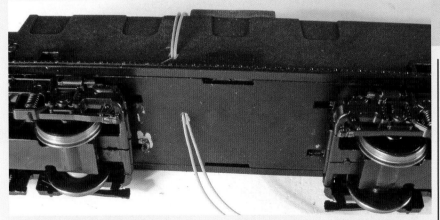

6 The speaker wires were threaded through to the underside - make sure they will not be visible through any side windows when the body is refitted.

7 Zimo recently introduced a mid-range 'stay alive' capacitor. At 20mm (27mm including tabs) x 15mm x 4.8mm this compact unit will store 6,800µF at 15V.

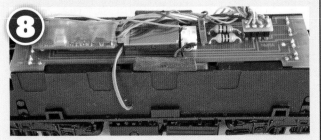

8 Connecting the capacitor is straightforward if you are able to solder. Attach the blue wire from the non-harness end of the decoder to the single tab on the capacitor. Likewise attach the grey wire to one of the paired tabs at the other end of the capacitor. I then plugged in the MX645R, twisted the harness to reduce its length securing the decoder and SC68 capacitor to the PCB with mastic.

9 No further work was required inside the model so I refitted the body. The speaker wires are in place to connect with a speaker housed in any of the possible ways. I demonstrated an ad hoc installation in HM83, so I chose to illustrate alternative solutions here.

10 DC Kits' cast resin enclosure was the first to be deployed. This comparison shot shows the resin unit, on the right, to be deeper than the Heljan original it is meant to replace, on the left.

11 It was very easy to use. I drilled a hole through which I passed the speaker wires and fixed it into position.

12 After soldering the wires to the speaker it was clipped into position. Corner fillets help to support the speaker and to block the fixing holes. That's all that is necessary, but I would probably fill in any gaps in a permanent installation, even though the underside is not visible during operation.

13 The alternative solution requires a little preparation. The Heljan moulding comprises four components. The outer two will be re-used so must be removed carefully to avoid breaking the locating pegs. Of the 12 pegs provided, I only managed to keep 11 intact!

14 The left and right-hand sides each fit one side of the enclosure only, so check the position of the locating holes carefully.

15 The mounting tabs fouled the slots in the chassis very slightly. I trimmed them to fit using a sharp blade.

16 Here you can see two tabs 'adjusted', the hole and longitudinal groove for the speaker wires, and the six locating holes for the side moulding attachment.

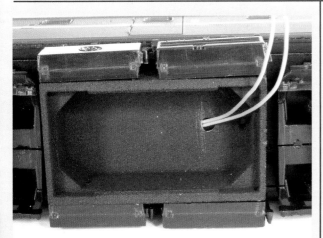

17 The enclosure has been fitted to the chassis with the speaker wires fed through. The retaining beads and corner fillets can be seen.

18 Finally, the speaker wires were attached and the speaker pressed into position.

Building the
CEMENT WORKS

Industry was the lifeblood of the railways, and can provide a reason for your model railway beyond passenger traffic. **MIKE WILD** explains how Felton Cement Works was developed using a readily available plastic kit as the basis.

CEMENT IS BIG BUSINESS for the railways, which even today sees bulk trainloads moved long distances by rail. With Felton Cement Works we wanted to represent a relatively small site that would handle short feeder trains of around eight wagons.

The cement works theme was chosen to provide an entirely different setting for one side of Shortley Bridge's extension – and to be something different from anything we had built before. The basis is a 6ft x 2ft baseboard while the buildings are from the Walthers Valley Cement plastic kit.

This kit is a superb method of creating a detailed cement works. We've made a number of modifications to it to allow it to fit our site properly including repositioning of the conveyor route, cutting one of the buildings in half to change its outward appearance and leaving the rear panels off other buildings so that low relief structures can be built from spare parts.

Assembling a kit like this can be daunting due to the large number of parts contained in the

box. The best method here is to work on one building at a time, assembling it carefully and following the instructions at all times.

In terms of tools you need no more than a basic tool kit comprising a craft knife and set of spare blades, a sanding board, liquid plastic cement and, as an option, superglue too. With

these items to hand there is nothing on this kit that can't be assembled and if you have built a wagon kit or small building before then it will present a great project.

The step by step guide shows the processes that we went through in order to create Felton Cement Works. ■

WHAT WE USED		
PRODUCT	**MANUFACTURER**	**CAT NO.**
Valley Cement	Walthers (Gaugemaster)	933-3098
Primer aerosol	Halfords	n/a
Plastic Magic liquid plastic cement	Deluxe Materials	AD-24
Grey shades weathering powders	DCC Concepts	DCW-GRY
Track weathering powders	DCC Concepts	DCW-TRK
Model filler	Humbrol	AE3016
1.5mm thick plasticard	Slater's	0160
Air dry clay	DAS	563746
Grey primer acrylic	Humbrol	1
4.5mm autumn static grass	MiniNatur	004-23
6.5mm autumn static grass	MiniNatur	006-33
4.5mm winter static grass	MiniNatur	004-24
6.5mm winter static grass	MiniNatur	006-34
Fine blended green turf	Woodland Scenics	WT1349
Coarse light green turf	Woodland Scenics	WT1363

A 'J39' 0-6-0 leads a mixed goods past Felton Cement Works as a 'K3' 2-6-0 simmers in the yard after arriving with set of empty wagons.

BUILDING FELTON CEMENT WORKS

1 The starting point for the cement works was a pair of Hornby Skaledale cement silos. Having established the track layout – see feature on pages 30-37 – the two silos were temporarily positioned on the layout.

2 To produce a realistic cement works we needed a large number of substantial buildings. The answer came in the Walthers Valley Cement kit supplied in UK by Gaugemaster. Even though it is based on an American prototype and to 'HO' (3.5mm:1ft) scale the kit holds great potential for a British scene too.

3 Having cut the bases for the main buildings from their sprues with a sharp craft knife they were laid out on the baseboard around the track layout. The bulk materials store (far right) is designed as a single building, but we planned to modify it by cutting it in half as a double frontage.

4 At the other end of the works we planned to use the cement silos and loading shed. The base was cut out first and positioned on the baseboard to ensure it would fit in the space available.

5 Construction then commenced with the loading shed – a critical component which establishes the positions of the silos and all other buildings. The plastic components are cleanly moulded and were bonded together with Deluxe Materials Plastic Magic applied with a small paintbrush.

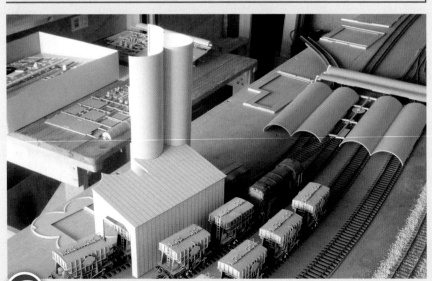

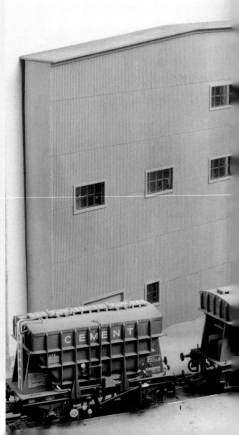

6 The cement silos were built up next. Take your time with these, ensuring all moulding pips are removed and that each section sets fully before adding the next.

7 The Walthers kit comfortably fills the 6ft length of this baseboard, particularly with the modifications to the materials store.

8 In order to fit in with the arrangement for Felton Cement Works, the position of the conveyor needed to be altered on one of the buildings. The opening on the front of the building is the intended position – we cut the new position out with a craft knife then blocked off the original with a piece of plain plasticard.

9 The cement roller crosses a track which will ultimately head out to an off scene siding. This is where we intend incoming coal traffic will be taken for the wagons to be unloaded. Fortunately the height of the roller is just enough to clear the roof of a Class 03 or 08 shunter.

10 Modifications to the materials store saw the base cut in half and the centre section removed to shorten it enough to fit alongside the railway. The two ends were then glued in place and sides trimmed to fit the new length. We saved one complete side from this building to use as a low relief building later in the build.

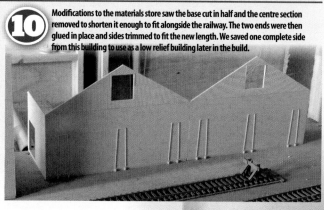

A Class 17 ticks over in the yard as a Class 08 draws loaded wagons through the loading shed.

BUILDING FELTON CEMENT WORKS

11 The track plan for the cement works caters for arriving trains of eight Presflo wagons and brake van. The train engine will be released allowing the works shunter to move the wagons into the sidings and through the loading shed. The size of the silos is apparent here.

12 The ground was built up between the cement works sidings and main running line to separate the two visually.

13

In this overview of the works the main buildings are all virtually complete with just the details for the silo tops remaining to fit. However, what you can't see is that the rear of the centre two buildings is missing, allowing the spare components to be used for extra low relief structures.

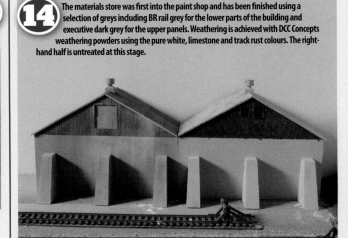

14 The materials store was first into the paint shop and has been finished using a selection of greys including BR rail grey for the lower parts of the building and executive dark grey for the upper panels. Weathering is achieved with DCC Concepts weathering powders using the pure white, limestone and track rust colours. The right-hand half is untreated at this stage.

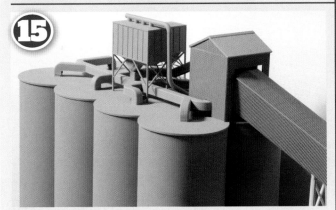

15

The top of the cement silos have been detailed now and painted with Halfords grey primer. This base colour was used throughout all other buildings except the materials store. Humbrol desert sand was also blown in lightly to add texture to the base colour of the buildings.

16

The buildings have all been weathered with DCC Concepts weathering powders using pure white, limestone and track rust colours. The difference between the weathered loading shed and the unweathered silos behind shows what a difference these powders can make.

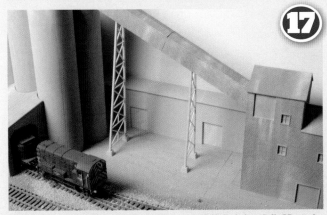

17

Two supports were cut to height to stand beneath the conveyor. Behind is the low relief building made from the spare materials store building side awaiting painting and weathering.

18

To give the low relief buildings more depth plain plasticard was used to make up 20mm deep sides while spare roof and conveyor sides were used to make roof panels. Humbrol filler was used to help smooth the edges – this was then sanded back once dry for a clean, smart joint at each corner.

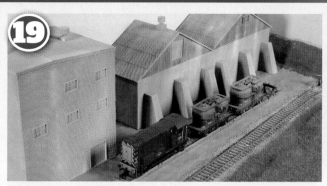

19 While the main exchange sidings are laid with traditional ballast, we wanted areas of the cement works to look like the track was bedded in with cement dust and mud. To do this we used DAS air drying clay. This was pushed in between the sleepers and underneath the edges of the buildings. The buildings were then placed back on top and pressed into the clay before it dried to mark their positions. After this they were removed again to allow the clay to dry thoroughly.

20 With the clay fully dry the buildings were replaced into their grooves and glued in place with contact adhesive. Next the clay base was painted grey with Humbrol primer acrylic No 1 as a base colour.

21 With the full base painted grey the works is really starting to take shape. The sleepers of the headshunt and other ballast sidings in the works were lightly dry brushed with the same grey primer colour to weather them slightly.

22 Next static grass was applied in carefully chosen areas around the trackbed to give the works a more detailed ground cover. Once dry hairspray was applied on top and Woodland Scenics fine blended green turf and light green coarse turfs were added carefully on top to increase the depth of the grass.

23 As a finishing touch the whole of the cement works base was brushed with varying levels of DCC Concepts limestone and pure white weathering powders. Mixing them together on the card meant the tone could be varied through the length of the works.

Modifying the buildings, including the materials store in the background, allowed the Valley Cement kit from Walthers to fill all of the available space at Felton Cement Works. A 'WD' 2-8-0 passes with empty cement wagons.

GRASS, BUSHES & TREES

Realistic grass and bushes make all the difference to the finished look of a model landscape. **MIKE WILD** explains his methods of creating the ground cover and details for Shortley Bridge and Felton Cement Works.

DEVELOPING the scenic aspects of a model railway is a really enjoyable part of a project, especially if you are armed with the right materials and a readiness to try different techniques.

The methods used for Shortley Bridge and Felton Cement Works are very similar to those we have used on past *Hornby Magazine* exhibition layouts and the result is grass with great texture and depth. However, you might be surprised to know that there is no secret or specialist skills involved in any of what you see here – it's just layers of materials built up on top of each other to create deep, rich, textured grass.

The first layer in any scenic project for us is Woodland Scenics fine blended turf and for a layout like this you will need a lot of it. We got through three large tubs building Shortley Bridge as it is used through all stages of the process. You will also need plenty of

PVA glue, a plentiful supply of brushes and, depending on the size of your project, several bags of MiniNatur static grasses or equivalent products from the Noch range supplied by Gaugemaster. Add to these coarse turfs from Woodland Scenics and a supply of the same manufacturer's fine leaf foliage and you have all the materials you need.

WHAT WE USED		
PRODUCT	MANUFACTURER	CAT NO.
Fine blended green turf	Woodland Scenics	WT1349
Light green coarse turf	Woodland Scenics	WT1363
Burnt grass coarse turf	Woodland Scenics	WT1362
Autumn static grass fibres, 4.5mm	MiniNatur	004-23
Autumn static grass fibres, 6.5mm	MiniNatur	006-33
Winter static grass fibres, 4.5mm	MiniNatur	004-24
Winter static grass fibres, 6.5mm	MiniNatur	006-34
Light green fine leaf foliage	Woodland Scenics	W1132
Olive green fine leaf foliage	Woodland Scenics	W1133
GrasMaster static grass applicator	Noch/Gaugemaster	60135
Extra hold hairspray	Various	n/a

Static grasses

Having established the first layer of fine blended turf (it may need a second application to ensure complete coverage), it is time to start adding the first layers of static grasses. Static grasses are fine fibres which when charged with static electricity will stand on end when they land on a layout. To achieve the best results »

A Thompson 'L1' 2-6-4T crosses the viaduct at the head of a set of Thompson non-corridor stock heading for Shortley Bridge.

with these a Noch GrasMaster or similar device is an essential tool and while this isn't a cheap item to purchase initially, the results are more than worth it.

The battery powered GrasMaster is loaded with static grass fibres and the cable is clipped to a metal component on the layout. Next the GrasMaster is switched on to apply a static charge to the fibres. Multiple layers of static grass can be applied using further diluted PVA glue, building up the depth and texture of the grasses.

While applying the static grass and with the glue still wet in each layer it is also worth dusting in a few pinches of Woodland Scenics fine blended turf. This again increases the depth and texture.

With all this done the really fun and creative part begins. Arm yourself with a can of extra hold hairspray, fine blended turf, coarse turfs in light and burnt grass colours. Working on a small area at a time, spray the ground textures with hairspray and then dust and work the various turfs into the static grasses. For even deeper

grasses small areas of static grass can be built up on top of this. This is a great time to experiment and the aim is to avoid the final grassed areas looking uniform.

Foliage and trees

We have found Woodland Scenics fine leaf foliage to be an invaluable material for scenic modelling. It isn't cheap, but it achieves impressive results quickly and without mess. It is supplied in boxes and we tend to make most use of the light green and olive green versions.

This material is supplied ready covered with coarse turfs over branches which look like small trees and bushes. They can be broken down into small pieces and planted around bridges and other structures allowing them to bed into their surroundings more realistically. We have also found fine leaf foliage handy for producing hedgerows alongside roads.

The trees on Shortley Bridge and Felton Cement Works are all proprietary items which have come from a number of sources including

the Model Tree Shop, International Models, Hornby and Woodland Scenics. The advantage of these is that they are ready to plant straightaway allowing quick assembly of these aspects, but that does come at a price.

Alternatives for trees including making your own from sea moss, plastic or metal tree armatures or scratch building trees from twisted wire as described in Nigel Burkin's series in *Hornby Magazine* – see HM83-HM85. The choice is yours.

Whatever route you choose to develop your scenery it should be an enjoyable experience. Don't be afraid to experiment. Take your time, step back and admire your work. And don't feel you have to produce the whole landscape in one go – there is always time to come back to enhance areas in the future too and that is something that we will definitely be doing with Shortley Bridge before its exhibition debut in November 2014 at the Warley National Model Railway Exhibition. ∎

A Class 17 rounds the curve through the bridge with a set of empty wagons bound for the cement works. The depth of the grass and the textures of the fine leaf foliage bushes are clear.

STEP -BY- STEP

REALISTIC GROUND COVER AND DETAILING

The basis of realistic grass textures is to work in layers. Having established the landscape and finished it with plaster bandage painted brown, the first layer to go down is Woodland Scenics fine blended green turf. This is applied over a layer of neat PVA glue spread with a damp paintbrush.

A single layer of fine turf isn't always enough to provide total coverage when working on larger areas. Here the excess material of the first layer has been collected for reuse, exposing bare patches of ground in the process.

To apply a second layer of fine turf use diluted PVA glue – we used a 60:40 ratio of PVA and water – and brush it over the ground surface.

This is then immediately covered with a second application of fine blended green turf. Once dry this the excess is removed and collected for reuse.

The solid base colour of blended green turf looks smart, but it doesn't have the texture that we want for realistic grasses. Mixing up a batch of diluted PVA glue with water to the same 60:40 ratio as before, the grass area was coated with glue. Next a Noch GrasMaster was loaded with MiniNatur autumn and winter fibres in a mixture of 4.5mm and 6.5mm lengths to create the effect shown in the left-hand side of this image.

The static charge applied to the static grass fibres makes them stand on end when they hit the layout, resulting in a deeper grass texture. However, one medium is not enough in our eyes and while the glue is still wet we dust in a few pinches of Woodland Scenics fine blended green turf which settles between the grass fibres to add depth. Multiple layers of static grass are important too – use a 40:60 PVA:water solution for a second layer of static grass.

Don't be afraid to make use of static grass around siding ends too – it's a great way of making the end of a line look unused. Be careful not to overdo this though as locomotives will find it difficult to negotiate large deposits of static grass, leading to erratic performance.

Having established the basic static grass finish across the layout it is now time to start adding detailing and building up the scenery layer upon layer. First to be tackled are the areas around the bridges. A great medium for bedding in structures like this quickly and effectively is Woodland Scenics fine leaf foliage. This can be broken up into pieces or used in clumps to represent bushes and shrubs.

Having established the boundaries of the road the next step is to build up the depth of the grass and increase its texture further. What you will need is extra hold hairspray, fine blended green turf, medium and burnt grass coarse turfs and potentially a small amount of static grass. Hairspray is then applied to the grass areas and the various turfs can be worked into it building up the layers and texture.

It's very much a trial and error process, but building up these layers of grass textures gradually will reap rewards. Here the main ingredients are fine and coarse turfs.

On the other side of the viaduct the final textures are more dedicated to static grasses with three layers being applied to create the effect of tall summer grasses growing alongside the railway.

Woodland Scenics fine leaf foliage is a very versatile material which can be very handy for blending structures into their surroundings. The road overbridge on the approach to the station doesn't look very settled at this stage with just static grass on the ground around it.

The hedgerows around the main road are all created with Woodland Scenics fine leaf foliage which helps to bed the road into its surroundings. It is the use of a layered approach to scenic detailing which achieves this final result.

13

By adding fine leaf foliage pieces around the wing walls the bridge can be bedded into its surrounding easily hiding any potential poor joins between the structure and the landscape.

14

Always check clearances when bedding in structures such as bridges. Trees and bushes growing over the railway can look effective, but they would never come into contact with rolling stock – at least, not for long!

15

Fine leaf foliage can also be used to create hedgerows alongside roads and railway lines. Break it up into small pieces and don't be afraid to use different colours for variation too – the outside world isn't a uniform green.

16

The finishing touches are trees. These can be used as highlights in open fields or, as here, to disguise a scenic break shielding the viewer's eye from areas that we don't want them to see. The trees on Shortley Bridge are from a number of sources including the Model Tree Shop, International Models, Hornby and Woodland Scenics.

Eastern Region Branch line
FORMAT

FROM 1948, the former London and North Eastern Railway (LNER) area was split in two South of the Scottish border following the formation of British Railways, creating the North Eastern and Eastern Regions. The two eventually merged again in 1967 to form one large Eastern Region.

There were many branch lines within these regions ranging from those that diverged from a station or junction on the main line and terminated at the end of a single track section to those that meandered across the country from one main line station to another with just a single track and passing loops along the way.

Our selection of 'OO' gauge branch line train formations includes services long and short from traditional passenger trains to longer holiday excursion trains heading for East Coast resorts. In the summer branch lines that served coastal resorts took on a new importance and came alive with an upsurge in passenger traffic, sometimes benefiting from a direct link with London or other major cities. Freight traffic was also an important factor and the pick up goods train was a staple of most branches. In later years enthusiast specials could be observed

and examples of these 'brake-van specials' have also been included to add a little extra variety.

When planning a branch line layout, always consider the maximum length of train you wish to run as there is nothing more frustrating than discovering your ideal trains are too long once the track has been laid! This was also important for the railway authorities with elements such as station size, number and length of platforms and length of run-round loops all taken into consideration before any work started. The position of points should also be planned according to your largest model locomotive, which in turn will allow the rest of your motive power roster sufficient clearance in headshunts and broaden operating potential.

If you are considering a branch line terminus, most would usually feature sidings for goods and storage purposes and would invariably include a headshunt to prevent fouling main running line. If you are planning an intermediate station, consider the layout of the station and access to the goods yard. Often, stations would feature a trailing siding that would require a locomotive to work forward and then reverse its wagons into the siding, having first detached the brake van in the station. Shunting operations would take place

in the yard before reforming the train, rejoining the running line and collecting the brake van before heading to the next calling point.

Eastern Region branch line operations have been increasingly well catered for by the main 'OO' gauge manufacturers in recent years with significant releases including Bachmann's Robinson 'J11' 0-6-0, Hornby's Thompson 'L1' 2-6-4T, Gresley and Thompson non-corridor suburban coaches together with an increasing selection of Diesel Multiple Units (DMUs) such as classes 101, 105 and 108 plus the Derby Lightweight sets and railbus types which gradually replaced steam.

Development work also continues on Hornby's forthcoming models of the Worsdell 'J15' 0-6-0 and Peppercorn 'K1', both of which could be found on forays along branch lines together with other larger designs such as Thompson 'B1' 4-6-0s and BR Standard '4MT' tank and tender engines. DJ Models' 'OO' gauge 'J94' 0-6-0ST is also in development while larger Eastern subjects are the focus

IONS

The Eastern Region of British Railways had a look and feel all of its own. **MARK CHIVERS** highlights a selection of branch line trains from the 1950s and 1960s.

for Heljan and DJ Models with development continuing on the Gresley 'O2' 2-8-0 and Raven 'Q6' 0-8-0 freight locomotives respectively.

'OO' gauge freight and coaching stock is also well represented with rolling stock available from the main manufacturers including Bachmann's versatile 16ton steel mineral wagons and a wide selection of 12ton ventilated vans together with Hornby's highly detailed BR 20ton brake van. Hornby's impressive new LNER extra-long Covered Carriage Truck (CCT) and Invicta Model Rail's BR Mk 1 CCT will allow parcels and other traffic to be modelled.

In coaching stock terms, Hornby offers Gresley 61ft 6in corridor coaches along with its new RailRoad range of BR Mk 1 coaches which would occasionally appear within a passenger rake as well as the more suited Gresley and Thompson non-corridor coaches. Suitable coaching stock from Bachmann's 'OO' gauge range includes its BR Mk 1 non-corridor stock, BR Mk 1 corridor and Thompson corridor coaches - new versions of the latter are currently being tooled.

The following is a list of suggested train formations representing a snapshot of 1950s/1960s era branch line train formations, researched from prototypical operations that can be replicated in model form using off-the-shelf products. ∎

A Bachmann BR '3MT' 2-6-2T leads a short three coach set of Hornby Thompon non-corridor stock around the curve from Felton Cement Works. This type of working was typical of Eastern Region branch lines, with changes of motive power depending upon which are the train was running in.

PASSENGER FORMATIONS

Hornby 'L1' 2-6-4T BR lined black (R3190),
two BR crimson Thompson Suburban BS.
LOCATION: Sandsend DATE: 1954

Hornby 'L1' 2-6-4T BR lined black (R3007), BR crimson Thompson Suburban BS/CL/S/S/BS.
LOCATION: Staithes DATE: 1957

Bachmann Ivatt '4MT' 2-6-0 BR lined black (32-585), BR crimson Thompson Suburban S/CL/S/S/BS.
LOCATION: Sandsend DATE: 1957

Bachmann Class 108 three-car DMU BR green, 'speed whiskers' (32-913).
LOCATION: Richmond (North Yorkshire) DATE: 1961

Bachmann Class 101 two-car DMU BR green, small yellow panels (32-286).
LOCATION: Newbiggin-by-the-Sea DATE: 1964

Hornby 'Black Five' 4-6-0 BR lined black (R2904), BR maroon BR Mk 1 BSK/CK/TSO/TSO/TSO/TSO/BSK.
LOCATION: Bridlington DATE: 1965

Bachmann Derby Lightweight two-car DMU BR green,
small yellow panels (31-537)
LOCATION: Aldeburgh DATE: 1966

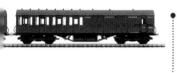

TYPE	LIVERY	MANUFACTURER	CAT NO.
12ton LMS cattle wagon	BR bauxite	Bachmann	37-704
16ton steel mineral with top flap doors	BR grey	Bachmann	37-225G
16ton steel mineral without top flap doors	BR grey	Bachmann	37-250H
16ton steel mineral pressed end door	BR grey	Bachmann	37-378
20ton hopper wagon	BR grey	Dapol	4F-034-007
20ton hopper wagon	BR grey	Hornby	R6564
BR 10ton insulated van	BR white	Bachmann	38-191B
BR 10ton insulated van	BR pale blue	Bachmann	38-190A
BR 12ton 'Insul-fish' van	BR white	Hornby	R6638
BR 12ton planked ventilated van	BR bauxite	Bachmann	38-161B
BR 12ton planked ventilated van (ply doors)	BR bauxite	Bachmann	38-231A
BR 12ton plywood ventilated van	BR bauxite	Bachmann	38-171C
BR 12ton plywood fruit van	BR bauxite	Bachmann	38-181C
BR 12ton shock absorbing van	BR bauxite	Bachmann	37-903A
BR 20ton brake van	BR bauxite	Bachmann	37-537A
BR 20ton brake van	BR grey	Bachmann	37-530
BR 20ton brake van	BR bauxite	Hornby	R6508
BR ZJO 'Trout' ballast hopper wagon	BR black	Hornby	R6622
Conflat A wagon with BD container	BR bauxite	Bachmann	37-951C
Eight-plank fixed end open wagon	BR grey	Bachmann	37-158C
Five-plank open wagon	BR grey	Bachmann	37-061C
NE 12ton ventilated van (corrugated ends)	BR bauxite	Bachmann	38-381
NE 12ton ventilated van (planked ends)	BR bauxite	Bachmann	38-376
NE 12ton van (corrugated ends)	BR bauxite	Bachmann	38-476
Seven-plank end door open wagon	BR grey	Bachmann	37-081F
Seven-plank fixed end open wagon	BR grey	Bachmann	37-107
Three-plank open wagon	BR bauxite	Bachmann	37-926A

Bachmann BR '3MT' 2-6-2T BR lined black (31-975), BR crimson Thompson Suburban BS, Gresley Suburban CL, Thompson Suburban BS. LOCATION: Levisham DATE: 1961

Hornby Class 31 BR green (R3144), BR maroon BR Mk 1 BSK/CK/SK/SK/SK/BSK. LOCATION: Hunstanton DATE: 1962

Two Bachmann Class 101 two-car DMUs BR green, small yellow panels (32-286). LOCATION: Saltburn DATE: 1967

GOODS FORMATIONS

Bachmann 'J11' 0-6-0 BR black (31-320DC), five-plank open wagon, 16ton steel mineral wagon, five-plank open wagon, two 16ton steel mineral wagons, BR 20ton brake van.
LOCATION: Birch Vale branch DATE: 1957

Bachmann 'J11' 0-6-0 BR black (31-319), two 16ton steel mineral wagons, LNER 12ton ventilated van, 12 ton ventilated van, BR 20ton brake van.
LOCATION: Dinting DATE: 1956

Bachmann 'J39' 0-6-0 BR black (31-855A), three-plank wagon, four LNER 12ton ventilated vans, two 16ton steel mineral wagons, BR 20ton brake van.
LOCATION: Settrington DATE: 1958

Bachmann 'J39' 0-6-0 BR black (31-855A), 12ton LNER ventilated van with corrugated ends, BR 20ton brake van.
LOCATION: Garton DATE: 1958

Bachmann 'J39' 0-6-0 BR black (31-865), three 16ton steel mineral wagons, BR 20ton brake van.
LOCATION: Alnwick DATE: 1962

Hornby Class 31 diesel BR green (R3144A), three BR 20ton brake vans BR bauxite, two five-plank open wagons, three BR 20ton brake vans.
LOCATION: Hadleigh (special working) DATE: 1962

Bachmann Class 24 diesel BR green, small yellow panels (32-430B), two 12ton ventilated vans, BR 20ton brake van.
LOCATION: Framlingham DATE: 1965

Bachmann 'WD' 2-8-0 BR black, late crests (32-252), six BR 20ton brake vans.
LOCATION: Tyne Docks branch (special working) DATE: 1965

Hornby Class 08 0-6-0 diesel shunter, BR green (R2872), three five-plank wagons, three 12ton ventilated vans, two 16ton steel mineral wagons, BR 20ton brake van.
LOCATION: Kelso DATE: 1965

Bachmann Ivatt '4MT' 2-6-0 BR lined black, late crests (32-585), 15 20ton coal hopper wagons, BR 20ton brake van.
LOCATION: Ashington DATE: 1967

'OO' EASTERN/NORTH EASTERN REGION BRANCH LINE LOCOMOTIVESS

CLASS	MANUFACTURER
LNER 'B1' 4-6-0	Bachmann
LNER 'C13' 4-4-2T	OO Works
LNER 'D11/2' 4-4-0	Bachmann
LNER 'D16/3' 4-4-0*	Hornby
LNER 'J11' 0-6-0	Bachmann
LNER 'J15' 0-6-0*	Hornby
LNER 'J39' 0-6-0	Bachmann
LNER 'K1' 2-6-0*	Hornby
LNER 'L1' 2-6-4T	Hornby
LNER 'N2' 0-6-2T	Hornby
LNER 'Q6' 0-8-0*	DJ Models
LNER 'V3' 2-6-2T	Bachmann
LMS 'Black Five' 4-6-0	Hornby
LMS Ivatt '4MT' 2-6-0	Bachmann
LMS Fairburn '4MT' 2-6-4T	Bachmann
BR '4MT' 2-6-0	Bachmann
BR '3MT' 2-6-2T	Bachmann
BR '4MT' 2-6-4T	Bachmann
Class 08	Bachmann/Hornby
Class 20	Bachmann
Class 24	Bachmann
Class 25	Bachmann
Class 26	Bachmann
Class 27	Bachmann
Class 31	Bachmann
Derby Lightweight	Bachmann
Class 101	Bachmann
Class 105	Bachmann
Class 108	Bachmann
Class 110	Hornby
Waggon und Maschinenbau Railbus	Heljan

Note: Locomotives marked with a * are currently in development.

'OO' READY-TO-RUN BRANCH LINE CARRIAGES

TYPE	LIVERY	MANUFACTURER	CAT. NO
BR Mk 1 Corridor Composite (CK)	BR maroon	Hornby/Bachmann	R4350/39-126
BR Mk 1 Corridor Second (SK)	BR maroon	Hornby/Bachmann	R4351/39-026
BR Mk 1 Open Second (SO/TSO)	BR maroon	Hornby/Bachmann	R4621/39-051
BR Mk 1 Corridor Brake Second (BSK)	BR maroon	Hornby/Bachmann	R4352/39-076
BR Mk 1 Suburban Brake Second (BS)	BR crimson	Bachmann	34-631
BR Mk 1 Suburban Composite (C)	BR crimson	Bachmann	34-703
BR Mk 1 Suburban Second (S)	BR crimson	Bachmann	34-609
BR Mk 1 Suburban Second Open (SO)	BR crimson	Bachmann	34-608
BR Mk 1 Covered Carriage Truck (CCT)	BR maroon	Invicta Model Rail	39-550Z
LNER Gresley Suburban Brake Second (BS)	BR crimson	Hornby	R4522A
LNER Gresley Suburban Composite with toilet (CL)	BR crimson	Hornby	R4521A
LNER Gresley Suburban Second (S)	BR crimson	Hornby	R4520A
LNER Gresley 61ft 6in Corridor Brake Composite (BCK)	BR maroon	Hornby	R4566
LNER Gresley 61ft 6in Corridor First (FK)	BR maroon	Hornby	R4567
LNER Gresley 61ft 6in Corridor Second (SK)	BR maroon	Hornby	R4568
LNER Thompson Suburban Brake Second (BS)	BR crimson	Hornby	R4577A/B
LNER Thompson Suburban Composite with toilet (CL)	BR crimson	Hornby	R4575A
LNER Thompson Suburban Second (S)	BR crimson	Hornby	R4576/A
LNER Thompson Corridor Second (SK)	BR maroon	Bachmann	34-378A
LNER Thompson Corridor Composite (CK)	BR maroon	Bachmann	34-403A
LNER Thompson Corridor Brake Composite (BCK)	BR maroon	Bachmann	34-428A
LNER extra long Covered Carriage Truck (CCT)	BR maroon	Hornby	R6683/A

USEFUL LINKS...

Bachmann	*www.bachmann.co.uk*
Dapol	*www.dapol.co.uk*
DJ Models	*www.djmodels.com*
Heljan	*www.heljan.dk*
Hornby	*www.hornby.com*
Invicta Model Rail	*www.invictamodelrail.com*

Review of the Year
2013-2014

Some spectacular new releases, surprise announcements galore and some hefty price rises made the last year one of the busiest ever in railway modelling. **MARK CHIVERS** looks back at the highlights since *Hornby Magazine Yearbook No 6*.

Hatton's of Liverpool's 'OO' gauge ready-to-run LMS Beyer, Garratt 2-6-0+0-6-2 was a highlight for many in 2014.

WHAT A YEAR it's been since *Hornby Magazine Yearbook No 6*! We've seen some amazing models, stunning announcements and a real sense of renewed popularity for railway modelling. It hasn't all been good, but we'll come on to those issues in a minute.

First, the good. And probably the most noticeable trend has been the number of new companies supplying ready-to-run models, backed by more recent entrants really finding

their feet. DJ Models recently announced another eight models to add to those announced last year, and Kernow Model Rail Centre switched its existing projects from Dapol to work directly with the manufacturing facility in China through an agreement with the company. This has enabled work to progress quickly on a number of models such as its 'OO' gauge London & South Western Railway (LSWR) Adams '02' 0-4-4T and PBA Tiger bogie china clay hopper. This also bodes well for its recently announced model of the Great Western Railway (GWR) '1361' 0-6-0ST.

Hatton's of Liverpool delivered a stunning

model to market earlier this year in the form of the London Midland & Scottish Railway (LMS) Beyer Garratt 2-6-0+0-6-2, a goliath of a locomotive. Produced by Danish manufacturer Heljan, it's proved popular and was significant in being Heljan's first British outline steam locomotive. Hatton's is not resting on its laurels and is working with DJ Models to produce a new GWR 'King' 4-6-0 locomotive for 'OO' with a raft of variants forming the initial batch of releases.

If that wasn't enough a number of new developments for model railways in the UK were announced during the year as Canadian

HM78, December 2013

HM79, January 2014

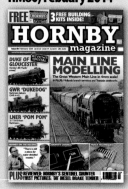
HM80, Febuary 2014

HM81, March 2014

HM82, April 2014

Bachmann's LYR '1008' 2-4-2T for 'OO'.

Hornby's 'OO' Sentinel 4wDH shunter.

manufacturer Rapido Trains unveiled its plan to produce its first 'OO' gauge model of a UK prototype in conjunction with Locomotionmodels using a manufactured-to-order business plan. This was soon followed by an announcement by DJ Models, and subsequently Kernow Model Rail Centre, that it was planning a 'crowd-sourcing' enterprise to allow production of a 'OO' Class 71 electric locomotive, as built for BR's Southern Region in 1958.

But it hasn't all been good. Some manufacturers have suffered issues with supply chain problems in China. Hornby, in particular, has suffered a torrid time over the past couple of years but the tide appears to be turning and with a new supply chain in place which doesn't rely on one main production facility, new products are beginning to arrive and in the quantity and quality we've come to expect. The company also has a new Chief Executive at the helm, following a period of uncertainty.

Bachmann has also suffered issues through the year, too, with the labour market in China proving particularly volatile. Factor in wage and welfare increases over the next five years and prices for models are going to be rising – in some cases significantly. Interestingly, the company announced that it was looking at ways to reduce the costs on models by cutting some of the manufacturing processes required for detail elements such as sprung metal buffers, for example. This comes at a time when Hornby has been considering the opposite and designing more detail back in to its models, as the perception was they had perhaps gone too far the other way.

As you'll see in our review whilst there has been some turbulence it's been a year that has brought much excitement to the hobby, too. »

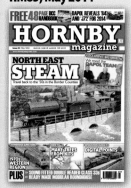

HM83, May 2014

HM84, June 2014

HM85, July 2014

HM86, August 2014

HM87, September 2014

OCTOBER 2013

The first month in review began with a stellar release from Hornby and its beautiful Great Western Railway 'Star' 4-6-0. Finished as 4018 *Knight of the Grand Cross* in GWR lined green it was clear the wait had been worth it for such a high standard model. It bristled with fine detail and performance was as exemplary as you'd hope from a model of one of the most important designs ever to take the rails.

Heljan also impressed with its 'O' gauge 'Western' in BR blue as D1048 *Western Lady*. Whilst this was Heljan's second attempt at a 'Whizzo', the first in 'OO', it was tooled from scratch and captured the impressive presence of the prototype.

Not to be outdone, Dapol released its production run of 'N' gauge 'Westerns' which started to arrive during the month and lived up to the impressive standard set by the limited edition model of D1000 *Western Enterprise* we'd seen in August.

October was a busy month for news, too. Expressions of interest were invited for *Hornby Magazine's* 'OO' gauge diesel brake tender which will appear in four liveries - plain BR green, BR green with small yellow panels and BR blue with yellow panels.

Hornby revealed its latest pre-production sample of the new 'N' gauge 'Brighton Belle' five car Electric Multiple Unit (EMU) at *Hornby Magazine's* inaugural Great Electric Train Show.

Locomotion, the National Railway Museum (NRM) at Shildon, unveiled the pretty little Lancashire and Yorkshire Railway (LYR) 2-4-2T

1008 in lined black livery as its latest model, while Invicta Model Rail announced a Class 419 BR Motor Luggage Van in BR blue, a pack of Network SouthEast liveried electric multiple unit translator vehicles and a set of three weathered departmental wagons in 'OO' for its exclusive limited edition range.

Australian based DCC Concepts launched Powerbase, designed to improve the haulage capacity of locomotives up gradients through the use of magnets and magnetic steel plates.

NOVEMBER 2013

Bachmann's 'OO' gauge LYR 2-4-2T arrived for review in November. Finished in BR lined black with early crests our sample immediately impressed. Nice finishing touches included the fully detailed cab interior and turned metal safety valves. Performance was spritely and surprisingly powerful: no surprise, then, that the model has proved popular.

Ixion released its fifth ready-to-run model - an 'O' gauge Fowler 0-4-0 diesel in GWR green. It had sprung buffers, three-link couplings, plenty of fine rivet detail, working headlamp and paint finish.

Turning to rolling stock, Hornby's new RailRoad range of 'OO' gauge BR Mk 1 coaches arrived including a Corridor Composite (CK), Corridor Second (SK) and a Brake Corridor Second (BSK) in BR maroon and BR chocolate and cream liveries. With a retail price of less than £18 the price may be budget but the model itself was very good indeed. Also fresh in from Hornby was its newly tooled Insul-fish van for 'OO'. Available in white and BR Express Parcels blue they captured the look of the prototype well with their distinctive heavy recessed doors though thankfully without the aroma of the real thing!

Bachmann was also busy on the rolling stock front during November with releases of the 'OO' gauge CovHop covered hopper wagons and GWR shunter's trucks. The Graham Farish range welcomed a set of 'N' gauge Bulleid coaches into the fold, finished in BR green and BR carmine and cream covering the Semi-open Brake Second, Open Second, Corridor Second and Corridor Composite.

Finally, Golden Age Models released its stunning handmade London and North Eastern Railway (LNER) Dynamometer Car in LNER teak finish featuring a fully detailed interior along with the distinctive measurement wheel beneath. Quality comes at a price, but worth every penny!

The Warley National Model Railway Exhibition at the NEC in Birmingham was held in November and generated plenty of news including Heljan's announcement of a GWR '1366' 0-6-0PT, a Metropolitan Railway Bo-Bo electric and a revised Class 33/0 diesel. Their display also included

After three years in the making Bachmann delivered its highly popular GWR 'Dukedog' 4-4-0 for 'OO'.

Hornby's GWR 'Star' 4-6-0 for 'OO'.

models at the development stage such as the 'OO' Class 26/0 diesel, AC Cars railbus and original condition 'Baby Deltic' while for 'O' gauge the English Electric Class 40 diesel locomotive looked impressive.

Bachmann displayed decorated samples of its 'OO' gauge Class 101 DMU, GWR '64XX' 0-6-0PT and LMS 57ft 'Porthole' coaches together with a selection of engineering prototypes (EP) of the revised Class 150 DMU and LMS 50ft Inspection Saloon in 'OO' together with its 'N' gauge Bulleid 'Merchant Navy' 4-6-2, BR Mk 1 CCT, Class 25/1 and Class 57/3 diesels.

Dapol's 'O' gauge Southern Railway (SR) 25ton Pillbox brake van and six-wheel milk tank were

also on display along with 'N' gauge samples of its Maunsell coaches, Maunsell Van C and Class 33/0 diesel.

Liverpool retailer Hatton's displayed a running sample of its forthcoming 'OO' gauge LMS Beyer-Garratt 2-6-0+0-6-2 locomotive at the exhibition and used *Hornby Magazine's* exhibition layout, Topley Dale, as a backdrop for the model during the weekend.

DECEMBER

December saw the arrival of Hornby's new 'OO' gauge BR '8P' 4-6-2 71000 *Duke of Gloucester* in BR lined green. The new '8P' definitely had the looks, poise and appearance of this unique

locomotive which also featured the first rendition in ready-to-run form of the British Caprotti valve gear. Straight from the box it ran smoothly and whilst clearly produced to retail at an affordable price, the verdict was that Hornby had done the locomotive proud and created a desirable, attainable and attractive model.

Hornby's Sentinel industrial diesel shunter was another impressive model to arrive for review. Its body shape was spot-on and it ran smoothly and consistently following a period of running in.

Bachmann's 'OO' gauge GWR 'Dukedog' 4-4-0 arrived for review, almost three years after it was first announced. The wait was definitely ≫

'OO' gauge Robinson 'J11' 0-6-0 by Bachmann.

worthwhile with our weathered sample capturing the old-fashioned and complex detailing of the 'Dukedog'. However, whilst the model ran smoothly and quietly straight from the box, three BR Mk 1 carriages in tow proved to be its limit whilst on test.

Bachmann's 'OO' gauge LNER 'J11' 0-6-0 in BR black also touched down in December and captured the prototype perfectly. Our review sample featured the later style smokebox door dart and Ross style safety valves.

Rolling stock wasn't forgotten either with the release of Hornby's new 'OO' gauge LMS Covered Carriage Trucks (CCT) and Bachmann's long-awaited 'OO' gauge model of the Polybulk covered bogie hopper wagon.

Hornby Magazine's newsdesk was busy throughout the run-up to Christmas, and the news was headed by the first pre-production sample of our new 'OO' gauge ready-to-run diesel brake tender model.

Decorated pre-production samples of Bachmann's 'OO' gauge Class 101 Diesel Multiple Units in BR green appeared, Kernow Model Rail

Centre issued the latest CAD/CAM drawings for its 'OO' gauge 'O2' 0-4-4T and Dapol updated *Hornby Magazine* on the current status of its new models including 'N' gauge SR 'Schools' 4-4-0 and rebuilt 'West Country'/'Battle of Britain' 4-6-2 locomotives, 'OO' gauge Class 73 and Class 121/122 railcars and 'O' gauge London, Brighton & South Coast Railway (LBSCR) 'Terrier' 0-6-0T, Class 08 diesel, SR 25ton 'Pillbox' brake van and six-wheel milk tanks.

Elsewhere, new entrant FTG Models announced plans to produce a 'OO' gauge model of the SPA air braked steel plate wagon via DJ Models, Invicta Model Rail added a set of weed control water tank TTA wagons to its list of exclusive models and retailer WH Smith announced it was bringing the Modelzone brand back to the high street at ten of its UK stores.

JANUARY

Bachmann's retooled Class 40 arrived in January and it was clear that the model was more refined than its previous incarnation with a reduction in the distance between the body

and the bogies, correct boiler exhaust position, operating directional lights and much more. Our DCC sound-fitted review sample also captured that oh-so distinctive whistling sound of the prototype well.

Heljan delivered the second of its trio of railbuses in 'OO' with the release of the AC Cars four-wheel railbus, the model exuding the look and charm of the real thing. The paint finish was first class and it ran beautifully too.

Hornby released two more versions of its GWR 'Star' 4-6-0 as 4061 *Glastonbury Abbey* in BR lined green with early crest and 4003 *Lode Star* in GWR lined green, the latter as an exclusive for STEAM – the Museum of the Great Western Railway. Both featured detail differences and demonstrated that Hornby's suite of tooling for the 'Star' is flexible enough to cover some of the myriad variations that affected this fleet.

For 'N' gauge, Bachmann released the Fairburn

Heljan's AC Cars railbus for 'OO'.

The new Class 25/1 for 'N' gauge from Bachmann.

Bachmann's upgraded Class 40 for 'OO'.

2-6-4T into its Graham Farish range. Our review sample was finished as Brighton built 42096 in BR black and it looked good from all angles. The first running sample of Heljan's 'O' gauge Class 60 diesel locomotive broke cover during January while engineering prototype samples of Bachmann's 'OO' gauge LBSCR 'E4' 0-6-2T and GWR '64XX' 0-6-0PT also appeared. In Margate, Hornby's newly tooled 'OO' gauge BR Mk 2E carriages arrived for evaluation by the company.

Kernow Model Rail Centre became the first model railway retailer to commission a limited edition model from DJ Models with the announcement of Hunslet 'Austerity' 0-6-0ST 196 *Errol Lonsdale* in Longmoor Military Railway blue livery for 'OO' gauge. Sheffield-based retailer Olivia's Trains commissioned Heljan to produce a limited run of 'OO' gauge Class 58 diesels and Bachmann unveiled a wide selection of 'OO' and 'N' gauge themed train packs and sets to celebrate 25 years of producing model railway products.

FEBRUARY

One of the most impressive ready-to-run models ever to grace the pages of *Hornby Magazine* arrived during February – Hatton's 'OO' gauge model of the LMS Beyer Garratt 2-6-0+0-6-2, produced by Heljan. Three years in the making, this stunning model captured the imposing stance of the prototypes to a tee. It looked the part and, most importantly, proved more than capable of hauling 100+ wagons while on test. You'd need a big layout ››

BR's unique '8P' 4-6-2 71000 *Duke of Gloucester* was immortalised in 'OO' by Hornby.

The smallest locomotive of 2014 – Bachmann's newly tooled 'N' gauge 'Jinty' 0-6-0T.

Arriving in July was Bachmann's new Midland '1F' 0-6-0T for 'OO'.

to really stretch its legs, but these models have appeared on layouts of all shapes and sizes. Quite right, too.

How could we follow that? How about Bachmann's 'N' gauge LMS 'Jinty' 0-6-0T, one of the smallest models released this year. It packed a lot into a tiny package. Yes, it was fine and delicate, but it was also comfortable to handle without fear of damaging it, with plenty of detail including glazed cab windows, sandboxes, outside brake rodding and even an engraving of the internal motion on the chassis under the boiler.

Heljan's first batch of retooled 'OO' Class 33/0 models also arrived for review. Featuring a brand new body, see-through roof fan grille and upgrades to the bogie details, our review model was a great improvement over the original release. The company also backdated its Class 23 Bo-Bo 'Baby Deltic' diesel to as-built condition and captured the stumpy 'nose' of the prototype with all the details where they should be including ladder, horn grille and correct lighting arrangement.

The Danish manufacturer also released the Class 128 diesel parcels unit in original Midland Region guise with four character headcodes and the former Western Region vehicles with gangway connections removed and headcode boxes plated over. Once again performance matched its good looks, no doubt helped in part by its heavy die-cast chassis.

Golden Age models impressed with its latest hand finished LNER 'Silver Jubilee' carriages in 'OO'. Finished in silver and chrome, each of the seven coaches was fully assembled by hand from metal components and featured extensive detailing inside and out.

In the news Bachmann displayed its first pre-production sample of the new 'N' gauge Maunsell 'N' 2-6-0 at Model Rail Scotland while Heljan displayed its forthcoming model of the 'OO' Park Royal railbus at the show, along with a selection

of its 'O' gauge wagons and a hand decorated sample of the Class 60 diesel.

Meanwhile, Kernow Model Rail Centre took delivery of its exclusive weathered 'N' gauge china clay wagon sets with both flat and tent style tarpaulins.

MARCH

Heljan's retooled 'OO' Class 33/0 in original condition arrived for review in BR green with full yellow ends. This version featured the as built exhaust silencer and engine bay cover fittings and offered an accurate original condition version of the class for the first time.

Olivia's Trains of Sheffield delivered something different in the form of Tinsley-based master and slave Class 13 diesel shunter in 'OO'. Produced using Bachmann or Hornby Class 08 donor models these custom-built locomotives captured the look of the distinctive (and for Olivia's Trains, local) prototypes well.

New rolling stock arrivals included 'OO' ex-LNER 10ton fish vans, Midland 20ton brake vans and PCA Metalair powder pressure discharge wagons from Bachmann together with a stunning 'OO' gauge resin cast roundhouse, reminiscent of the one at Par in Cornwall from Kernow Model Rail Centre.

In the news, Dapol announced its plans for the coming year with a new North Eastern Railway (NER) Worsdell 'J72' 0-6-0T for 'N' gauge, a Vossloh Class 68 Bo-Bo diesel for 'N' and 'OO' and Southern Railway Adams 'B4' 0-4-0T in 'OO'. The company also revealed a plethora of new liveries for its existing toolings.

Bachmann lifted the lid on the contents of its special Silver Anniversary Set in 'OO' and 'N' marking 25 years of model railway manufacturing in the UK. The special wooden boxed set comprised Class 47 47164 in BR blue with Union flags and 'Jubilee' 4-6-0 45552 *Silver Jubilee* in BR green with early crests. The company

also updated progress on its new 'N' gauge Class 25/1 and 25/2 diesels together with the first engineering prototype of its new BR 22ton Tube wagon for 'OO'.

Rail Exclusive unveiled colourful plans to recreate the contemporary 'Northern Belle' luxury train livery on a pair of ViTrains 'OO' gauge Class 47s while Heljan issued the first images of its 'OO' gauge model of the London Transport Metropolitan Railway Bo-Bo, highlighting progress to date. There was a departure of huge significance too when Marketing Manager Simon Kohler left Hornby Hobbies at the end of March after 35 years with the company following a reorganisation of the Marketing Department. Recognised by thousands of modellers as the face of Hornby, Simon left to set up his own company and has continued to support the Margate-based manufacturer.

APRIL

The *Hornby Magazine* office witnessed 'Deltics' large and small during April with examples arriving for review from LH Loveless in 'O' and Bachmann in 'N' gauge – and it was clear that none of the models were made by fools.

Both immediately caught our attention, the Loveless handmade all-metal model's impressive proportions captured the scale and presence of the English Electric diesels superbly, offering a substantial model that feels and looks like the prototype and bristling with detail inside and out.

The 'N' gauge Graham Farish model was equally impressive. The overall shape and feel of the body was good with all the important curves, lines and shapes just how they should be. Bachmann also delivered a centre-headcode version of its retooled 'OO' gauge Class 40 diesel.

In the news, Hornby offered a glimpse of its new LNER 'J15' 0-6-0, FTG Models showed off decorated samples of its 'OO' BR SPA plate wagon in BR Railfreight red livery and Heljan added two Cargowaggon vehicles to its 'O' gauge range.

Finally, Bachmann announced price rises across the board on its range of model railway products, citing labour and raw material costs as the main drivers. Although there was widespread disappointment at the price hike, there was also recognition that Bachmann was acting out of necessity rather than greed.

MAY

May saw the arrival of Bachmann's long-awaited 'OO' gauge Class 101 DMU for review. Finished in original BR green livery with straw lining and 'speed whiskers', the model looked the part straight from the box with plenty of exquisite detail evident and it ran exceptionally well too.

Heljan's newly tooled original condition Class 26/0 for 'OO'.

Original condition 'OO' gauge 'Baby Deltic' from Heljan.

Heljan's backdated original condition Class 33/0 for 'OO'.

Bachmann delivered its new 'OO' gauge Class 101 DMU.

Previously only available in later condition with smooth cab fronts and later exhaust positions, Heljan's 'OO' gauge Class 26 diesel finally arrived in as built condition featuring original cab front communication doors, cabside quarter lights with straight frames, original exhaust position and original style bogies.

For 'N' gauge, Dapol released its Doncaster-built version of the Class 56 as 56090 in large logo blue livery which proved capable of hauling a 25 wagon train with ease.

Bachmann's 'OO' gauge 57ft 'Porthole' coaching stock also caught our attention with the Open First and Corridor Third variants arriving for review. Finished in BR carmine and cream they featured frosted 'Portholes', handles, grabrails, steps, brackets, gangways and separately fitted filler pipes. Curiously, the bogies also featured pick ups on all wheels – interior lighting for the future, perhaps?

The first images of Hornby's BR Peppercorn 'K1' 2-6-0 and LNER extra long CCT van looked promising - the 'Mogul' appearing particularly impressive. Heljan also confirmed the identities of its 'OO9' Lynton and Barnstaple Manning Wardle 2-6-2Ts as 759 *Yeo*, 760 *Exe* and 761 *Taw* as well as identities for its new 'OO' Class 05 diesel, Class 35 'Hymek', LNER/BR 'O2' 2-8-0, Park Royal railbus and Metropolitan Railway electric locomotive.

JUNE

June was a quieter month for new locomotives although there were plenty of re-liveried models arriving including Bachmann's 'OO' Class 101 in BR blue and grey, Dapol's latest 'N' gauge BR '9F' 2-10-0 in BR black and a sublimely weathered 'Western' in 'N'.

On the rolling stock front, Dapol's newly-tooled 'O' gauge Southern Railway 25ton 'Pillbox' brake van rolled in. Available initially in four liveries the model featured standard even planking for the van body and correctly profiled roof edge. It also featured separately applied metal handrails and lamp irons, sprung metal buffers, brass bearing pockets, glazing and pre-fitted brake rigging.

Bachmann's 57ft 'Porthole' Corridor Brake Third in BR carmine and cream also arrived for review and followed the high standard laid down by the previous releases.

The newsdesk was running full tilt, which was a good job when Rapido Trains surprised everyone with its plans for a 'OO' gauge model of the Advanced Passenger Train – Experimental (APT-E), produced in conjunction with Locomotionmodels and the National Railway Museum (NRM). It will be available as a prototypical four-car set, with an additional trailer car offered for those who wish to lengthen the formation and will feature a fully detailed interior, lighting and tilt mechanism.

Hornby's first pre-production sample of the new Holden 'D16/3' 4-4-0 arrived for evaluation with the company together with a second »

'Deltics' for 'O' gauge and 'N' gauge arrived through Lovelass and Bachmann in April.

The all new Fairburn 2-6-4T for 'N' gauge from Bachmann's Graham Farish brand.

sample of its Drummond '700' 0-6-0. Both models were due for release as the Yearbook went to the printers in October.

Kernow Model Rail Centre received the first running sample of its 'OO' gauge 'O2' 0-4-4T. Rapid progress had been made on the project since the company started working directly with the factory in China.

Dapol continued to stride ahead displaying an engineering sample of its 'O' gauge LBSCR Stroudley 'Terrier' 0-6-0T and the first shots of its eagerly awaited 'OO' gauge Class 73/0 electro-diesel locomotives.

Bachmann's 'OO' gauge LMS 50ft Inspection Saloon edged ever closer with decorated samples arriving for inspection along with liveried samples of Invicta Model Rail's exclusive BR Mk 1 Covered Carriage Trucks (CCT).

Finally, following the success of its 'OO' gauge version Heljan announced plans to produce a ready-to-run 'O' gauge model of the Brush prototype diesel D0280 *Falcon*.

JULY

'Half cab is no half measure', read the headline in the review section and that was certainly true of the 'OO' gauge Midland '1F' 0-6-0T from Bachmann. The model immediately impressed, the company managing to capture the stature of this purposeful looking locomotive perfectly. Another top quality model from Bachmann, in its 25th anniversary year.

Bachmann's new 'N' gauge BR Sulzer Type 2 D5222 in weathered BR green livery arrived for review and looked the part. The model captured the looks of these locomotives and, again, featured plenty of exquisite detail including crisply moulded gangway doors, flush glazed windows, separately fitted handrails and buffers, boiler port and roof fan grille. The model even has separately fitted sandboxes and steps on the bogies – in 'N' gauge!

Bachmann's LMS 50ft Inspection Saloon in 'OO' also arrived for review, and proved to be well worth the wait. Our sample was finished in BR maroon as M45020M and captured the look of the prototype to perfection. Decoration was flawless and the model featured a wealth of detail including separately fitted filler pipes and handrails, battery boxes, vacuum brake cylinders, propane storage tank and a finely produced set of folded steps. Inside the model features moulded tables and chairs and is just crying out to be populated.

July heralded Bachmann's 25th anniversary celebrations with new product announcements including a range of 'OO9' scale models. The company plans to produce a ready-to-run Baldwin Class 1-12-D 4-6-0T in four liveries together with a covered bogie wagon and three-plank bogie open wagon to complement it. The company is also producing a Class 90 electric in 'OO' together with two FFA/FGA Freightliner container flats. A set of South Eastern and Chatham Railway (SECR) 'Birdcage' carriages for 'N' gauge completed the new tooling announcements. A wide selection of re-liveries on existing tooling was also unveiled in the new 'N' and 'OO' catalogues from Bachmann Europe.

In celebration of its first year of trading DJ Models announced eight new models in July including the much requested Raven 'Q6' 0-8-0, a Hudswell Clarke 0-6-0ST and a Class 59 diesel in 'N' and 'OO' together with a Southern Region Class 71 Bo-Bo electric locomotive in 'OO'. Completing the line-up for 'N' gauge is a new model of the GWR '63XX' 2-6-0. The Class 71 announcement is particularly interesting as it involves a 'crowd sourcing' enterprise to fund the project and push it forward.

Whetting the appetite, Hornby's new Crosti-

boilered '9F' 2-10-0 arrived at the manufacturer's Margate headquarters for assessment during July, a set of exclusive pictures appearing in *Hornby Magazine's* news pages. The Crosti '9F' is set for release in Hornby's RailRoad range.

Finally, Locomotionmodels unveiled its new 'OO' gauge ready-to-run model of the NRM's Great Northern Railway (GNR) Ivatt 'C1' 4-4-2 251. Manufactured by Bachmann, it will be the tenth 'OO' gauge model in its National Collection in Miniature series. Three versions will be available and delivery is expected later this year.

AUGUST

Hornby's new and eagerly anticipated 'OO' gauge Gresley 'P2' 2-8-2 2001 *Cock O' the North* in LNER apple green arrived in shops at the end of August. This first release was the RailRoad version with reduced decoration but the model still makes use of the same tooling as the main range version. First impressions were good, the model capturing the look of the prototype well - and on test it ran incredibly smoothly too. The main range 'P2' was due during September along with the Twin Track Sound version, which features Hornby's new budget DCC sound decoder.

Hatton's of Liverpool also delivered another batch of its 'OO' gauge LMS Beyer Garratts, this time featuring the distinctive oscillating bunker which offered easier access to the coal supply for the fireman. Another impressive release produced for Hatton's by Heljan.

The Danish manufacturer also issued a fourth variant of its popular Class 128 parcels railcar, which this time offered the unit in Western Region condition without headcode boxes but retaining the gangway connections in Royal Mail red livery and BR blue.

On the rolling stock front, Dapol delivered its 'O' gauge six-wheel milk tank wagons. Available in six liveries the model was based on an LMS type although produced to a generic design by Dapol. Hornby's 'OO' BR Mk 3 coach also gained an upgrade with interior lights fitted for the first time

in the BR blue and grey liveried versions.

Kernow Model Rail Centre announced its intention to manufacture a 'OO' gauge model of the GWR '1361' 0-6-0ST. Produced through DJ Models, five variants will form the initial releases. Meanwhile, Bachmann used its annual Collector's Club day at the Keighley and Worth Valley Railway to announce a new 'OO' gauge Webb 'Coal Tank' 0-6-2T for release in 2016. Shortly after, Hatton's of Liverpool revealed its plans to produce a 'OO' gauge GWR 'King' 4-6-0, in 14 variants, through DJ Models. GWR enthusiasts have been waiting a long time for a really up to date 'King' and this is going to be very popular, we feel.

Finally, a second engineering sample of *Hornby Magazine's* diesel brake tender arrived for evaluation featuring brand new bogie toolings together with numerous improvements and adjustments.

THE ROAD AHEAD

Who would have thought a few years ago that a retailer would produce a model that has become the standout release of the past year? For me and many others, Hatton's 'OO' gauge LMS Beyer Garratt 2-6-0+0-6-2 was the highlight - a stunning model.

Coming up in addition to all the models announced, the DJ Models/Kernow Model Rail Centre 'crowd sourcing' enterprise could potentially be a groundbreaking development in funding models which haven't yet made it onto the drawing board. Potential customers have to pay up front before production can start, but if it makes hitherto overlooked models viable then that's got to be good. If it does take off, expect some real surprises to be announced.

We've seen Digital Command Control become ever more popular and that shows no sign of changing - and with budget DCC sound fitted models from Hornby due in the not too distant future, and lots of other projects in the pipeline, there are exciting times ahead for this hobby of ours. ■

GWR shunter's trucks for 'OO' from Bachmann.

Golden Age Models LNER dynamometer car, handbuilt in brass in 'OO' scale.

Hornby's new RailRoad Mk 1 carriage family for 'OO'.

BR 'Covhop' wagons for 'OO' from Bachmann.

'Polybulk' grain hopper from Bachmann in 'OO'.

Midland 20ton brake van for 'OO' from Bachmann.

LMS 'Porthole' carriages from Bachmann for 'OO'.

Dapol's 'O' gauge SR 'Pillbox' 25ton brake van.

Arriving at the very end of August was the first of Hornby's three versions of the fabulous Gresley 'P2' 2-8-2. This is the RailRoad version…

COCK O' THE NORTH

The BR Type 2
DIESELS

One of the most noticeable results of the 1955 Modernisation Plan was the appearance of a large number of medium power Type 2 diesels, some of which were extremely long lived. **EVAN GREEN-HUGHES** looks at the rise and fall of these popular machines.

BR Suzler Type 2 D5278 leads a rake of empty limestone hoppers past Stanier 'Black Five' 4-6-0 45083 on the approach to Gowhole sidings in 1965. Alan Bryant/www.railphotoprints.co.uk.

AS THE UK EMERGED from the Second World War the country was locked into a financial crisis which crippled it for years. Much of the money which had been spent fighting the enemy had been borrowed from allies such as America and had to be paid back, while at home industry was struggling to cope with the contractions forced on it by the secession of hostilities.

During this period the Government had to operate a strict balance of payments policy, which meant using home-grown or home-built products in preference to imports and this in turn impacted on the amount of oil which the country could bring in. From the railway's point of view this meant that there was a great deal of pressure to find ways of providing power from home produced coal, rather than by using imported energy.

British Railways, therefore, continued to build steam locomotives while its master, the British Transport Commission (BTC), debated how best to pay for an electrified railway which could be powered by energy generated from power stations burning home dug coal. Within a few years it quickly became apparent that the capital required to provide large scale electrification was not going to be available. By this time the railway's losses were spiralling out of control with one of the contributory factors being the high cost of operating steam engines.

By 1955 the situation had changed sufficiently for the BTC to publish its Modernisation Plan, the central plank of which was the replacement of the steam engine by more efficient diesel and electric equivalents. By then the balance of trade situation was not so critical, the economy was in a better place and there was a need to reduce pollution and improve cleanliness.

The original plan provided for a gradual replacement process with new diesels taking the place of steam on like-for-like duties. To enable this to take place small batches of diesels would enter service for evaluation with a full scale programme to follow once the performance of the first batch had been analysed.

At this stage it was imagined that three power groups for diesels would be required, excluding shunters and self-propelled units. The first, to be called Type A, covered locomotives of up to 1,000hp and equated to steam locomotives with the power classifications 1 and 2. The second, the Type B, was to be the most numerous and would cover engines of between 1,000 and 1,250hp with performance something like a Class 3 steam locomotive while the third group, Type C, was for locomotives of over 2,000hp and was described as being for heavy traffic, although in reality these would only be a match for a modern Class 7 steam locomotive at best.

It wasn't long before these categories were modified and, hardly surprisingly, the Type B's range was expanded to encompass 1,000hp to 1,499hp from which point the type was »

rechristened as the Type 2. What was particularly surprising was that there was no specification for a more powerful type with a pulling power matching the then current crop of useful mixed traffic steam engines. In this category were the London Midland & Scottish Railway 'Black Five' which produced about 25,000lbs tractive effort, the Great Western Railway's 'Hall' which offered 27,000lbs and the Southern's 'Merchant Navy' with a whopping 33,000lbs. Riddles' standard mixed-traffic designs had carried on the good work with the '4MT' 4-6-0s coming in at 25,000lbs and with a similar figure being available from the versatile 2-6-4Ts.

Given that information it is therefore a little surprising that the British Transport Commission chose to purchase so many replacement locomotives in the Type B bracket for, with the technology available at that time, these would only provide the equivalent power to something like a Midland '3F'. It was perhaps typical of the dysfunctional railway of that time that the very work for which this power group was intended was rapidly declining while no provision was made for high powered locomotives which could accelerate express trains or which would be suitable for use on heavy bulk freight.

Initial batches

In the mid-50s British Railways' own workshops had limited experience of working with diesels and the BTC therefore decided that batches of locomotives should be ordered from several of the independent companies which were engaged in such work as well as from railway workshops. It would dearly liked to have been able to order some from America as well, for that was where the experience lay at that time, but such proposals were very firmly turned down by a government which was fearful both of its balance of trade position and also of the unions and workers in its state industries.

While British Railways laid out the general arrangement of the Type Bs the actual detail design was decided by the contractors. All were intended for mixed traffic duties and were to be fitted with a cab at each end, the number of wheels was not specified but the axle weight was not to exceed 18.75tons, a steam heat generator was to be fitted and the completed locomotive was to be capable of working trains at up to 75mph.

Several manufacturers expressed interest in constructing the new locomotives with one of the front runners being the railway's own works at Derby. There were those in the BTC who would have awarded the whole order to this source so that the work could be kept within the railway's own workshops, but others insisted that batches should be obtained from elsewhere for comparison purposes.

Derby came up with a compact locomotive which was just over 50ft long, mounted on two four-wheel bogies with all axles powered. The 1,160hp six-cylinder power unit came from Sulzer while the main generator and the traction motor came from British Thomson-Houston, a company which already had extensive experience in the supply of electrical equipment for railway use.

Due to the limited power available from such locomotives double-heading was likely to occur at regular intervals and as a result the BTC decreed that locomotives should have nose end doors with corridor connections so that the crews could get from one to another should this

BRITISH RAILWAYS TYPE B (TYPE 2) DIESEL LOCOMOTIVES							
BUILDER	TOPS CLASS	YEAR	NO MADE	BOGIES	HORSE-POWER	WEIGHT	LENGTH
North British	21**	1958	58	Bo-Bo	1,100	72t 10cwt	51ft 6in
North British	22	1958	58	Bo-Bo	1,100	65t 0cwt	46ft 8in
English Electric	23	1959	10	Bo-Bo	1,100	73t 17cwt	52ft 6in
BR Derby	24	1958	151	Bo-Bo	1,160	73t 0cwt	50ft 6in
BR Derby	25	1961	327	Bo-Bo	1,250	73t 0cwt	50ft 6in
BRCW	26	1958	47	Bo-Bo	1,160	73t 6cwt	50ft 9in
BRCW	27	1961	69	Bo-Bo	1,250	73t 6cwt	50ft 9in
Metropolitan Vickers	28	1958	20	Co-Bo	1,200	97t 3cwt	56ft 7in
Brush	31*	1957	263	A1A-A1A	1,365	104t 0cwt	56ft 9in

*Originally Class 30.   **Class 29 was the re-engined Class 21.

Note: All locomotives listed above are diesel electric except Class 22 which used diesel hydraulic transmission.

be required when operating in multiple. This, along with an array of bodyside grilles gave what was to become the Class 24 a rather cluttered appearance.

Though largely successful there were complaints that the end doors made the cabs draughty and that the braking system was not as efficient as it might have been, something which led to a ban on using the class in certain areas on loose coupled trains. Later on an intercooled engine was used in the successor Class 25, which gave another 100hp, and the bodyside design was revised to group all the grilles at the top of the body sides. Some were geared for 90mph running and a redesigned cab sorted out many of the crew issues. This class eventually totalled 477 examples and was largely successful.

The workhorses

The Class 24/25 family as they were to become eventually was to find work all over the system hauling everything from local passenger trains to long-distance freight. Rugged and reliable they were only to face withdrawal as a result of their original design failings when they were superseded by much more powerful classes which were capable of moving heavier loads at higher speeds. Nevertheless the first one didn't go until 1974 and the last was not taken out of service until 1987.

For comparison purposes with the Derby in-house design, the Birmingham Railway Carriage and Wagon Company was given an order to produce the first 20 of what was later to become the 116-strong Class 26/27 family. Mechanically these followed closely the BR design, being fitted with the same Sulzer engine, but with Crompton Parkinson electrical gear. The design of these Type Bs was rather more pleasing than the BR product as a stylish cab constructed from glass fibre was fitted and the ventilation grilles were grouped together on the cantrail leaving an uncluttered body side.

The first examples, delivered in 1958, were two tons above the design weight, but the class was taken straight into service and was just as reliable as the BR-built version. Further refinements decreased the weight and an improved power unit from D5347 onwards brought power output up to 1,250hp. These later locomotives were eventually classified as Class 27 and were fitted **»**

With its steam heating working hard, BRCW Sulzer Type 2 26010 prepares to leave Edinburgh Waverley for Carstairs with a mail train on February 19 1979.
John Chalcraft/*www.railphotoprints.co.uk.*

25067, now with its cab communication doors welded up, rattles through Horbury Cutting as it approaches Healey Mills with a local trip freight working on September 11 1981. *www.railphotoprints.co.uk.*

The Metropolitan Vickers Co-Bo diesels were one of the failures of the pilot scheme. In 1959 D5702 heads away from Disley Tunnel with a Manchester-Derby working.
Alan Bryant/*www.railphotoprints.co.uk.*

With single CCT and GUV behind, Class 24 5013 approaches Carnforth in August 1970. Mike Jefferies/*www.railphotoprints.co.uk.*

Carrying large logo grey and with modified cab fronts, Class 26 26006 joins the ECML at Prestonpans with coal from Blindwells opencast to Cockenzie Power Station as an up East Coast Main Line HST passes in the background on March 9 1987. John Chalcraft/*www.railphotoprints.co.uk.*

MODEL BR TYPE 2S – 'OO' GAUGE		
CLASS	MANUFACTURER	STATUS
Class 21	Dapol	In production
Class 22	Dapol	Available
Class 23	Heljan	Available
Class 24	Bachmann	Available
Class 25	Bachmann	Available
Class 26	Heljan	Available
Class 27	Heljan	Available
Class 28	Hattons	Available
Class 29	Dapol	In production

North British diesel hydraulic Type 2 6334 shunts china wagons stock at Torrington on August 27 1971.
John Medley/www.railphotoprints.co.uk.

North British Type 2 D6150 runs into Aberdeen from Fraserburgh on July 21 1965. This class was re-engined to create Class 29, but nevertheless all were still withdrawn by the end of 1971.
Sid Rickard/www.railphotoprints.co.uk.

with GEC electrical equipment due to Crompton Parkinson being fully committed to supplying parts for the new 'Peak' Class Type Cs. Interestingly the original BRCW product was marginally more powerful than a Class 24 and could turn out 25,000lbs continuous tractive effort.

Although they had a wide sphere of operation the BRCW locomotives found their spiritual home in Scotland where they worked singly and in pairs for many years. They faired well in the culls which arose when BR realised that it had far too many low horsepower locomotives available and were not withdrawn en masse until the mid 1980s, with the last one not being taken out of service until 1993.

Six axles

While the Sulzer-engined locomotives proved to be very successful there were a number of other Type Bs which were to prove costly failures. Some were re-engineered to become useable but others were to be scrapped long before they should have been due to their defective design or poorly-performing components.

It may surprise some readers that the Brush Traction A1A-A1A Type B is mentioned at this point. This is a very well-known and well-loved locomotive which has had a very long and successful life. What is not so well known is that when these machines were first constructed they were equipped with a Mirrlees JVS12T power unit which provided only 1,250hp, and that they then fell very firmly into the Type 2 category.

The Brush locomotive took the Type B specification to another level. It was more powerful than either the original Derby or the Birmingham product and its makers intended it to be a match for mixed traffic 4-6-0s in the Class 5 category. Weighing in at 104tons it had to be carried on two six wheel bogies, with the centre axle on each unpowered in order to meet BR's axle weight specification. Design consultants were brought in to improve the looks of the locomotive, which they certainly did, and the whole package looked very promising.

Unfortunately when the first batch was put to work on the Great Eastern section's Liverpool Street-Clacton turns in 1957 they had to be worked very hard to match the performance of the steam locomotives which they had replaced, resulting in a number of failures. By this time a second batch had already been ordered, but fitted with a 1,365hp version of the Mirrlees engine and electro-pneumatic control

instead of electro-magnetic as in the first batch. Subsequent upgrades saw the Mirrlees engine delivering 1,600hp and eventually 263 of these locomotives were at work. Unfortunately metal fatigue problems soon emerged with the Mirrlees equipment - particularly with the engine castings - and this seemed to directly relate to efforts to extract more power as the original low-powered machines were never affected in the same way.

After battling the problem for some time British Railways embarked on a radical solution and began to remove the Mirrlees engines and replace them with English Electric 12SVs downrated to 1,450hp to match the original electrical equipment. Thus modified the Class 31s went on to be one of the more successful classes, many being subsequently fitted with electric train heating equipment and air brakes. Most lasted well until the 1980s 'Sprinter' revolution and there are still a few working today, both on the main line and in preservation.

The failures

While the Brush machines were successfully modified to give long service the same cannot be said for the 58 1,100hp diesel-electric Type Bs supplied by the North British Locomotive Company. These were supplied with power units based on the German MAN design and electrical equipment by GEC. From the outset there were problems with the coupling between the engine and generator and the rather weedy engine could not cope with the allocated duties on the Great Northern suburban lines out of London. Reliability issues led to the class being reallocated to Scotland, so that they could be near their builder, but NBL folded in 1962 leaving support for the class sadly lacking.

With reliability figures far beneath those of the equivalent Derby and Birmingham Type Bs drastic action was proposed and subsequently there was a plan to fit Paxman Ventura engines. However, only 20 were rebuilt before the National Traction Plan proposed concentration on the larger classes and subsequently all were withdrawn at the end of 1967, some after a life of less than 10 years.

NBL also produced a diesel-hydraulic version of its locomotive, which was slightly more successful, largely because it weighed nine tons less. Basically similar to the diesel-electric design, apart from the transmission, it suffered from the same problems with the power unit which proved a major problem after the demise of its makers. **»**

MODEL BR TYPE 2S – 'N' GAUGE

CLASS	MANUFACTURER	STATUS
Class 22	Dapol	Available
Class 23	DJ Models	In production
Class 24	Bachmann	Available
Class 25	Bachmann	Available
Class 26	Dapol	Available
Class 27	Dapol	Available
Class 31	Bachmann	In production

Right: **The higher powered Class 27 built by BRCW was a direct follow up to the Class 26. Class 27/1 27109 heads away from Burntisland with the 10.17am Dundee-Edinburgh in June 1983.** John Chalcraft/*www.railphotoprints.co.uk.*

Below: **The Derby-designed Sulzer Type 2s, later Class 24, were one of the great successes of the pilot scheme. Class 24 D5015 stands alongside Fowler '4F' 44088 - one of the steam designs the new diesels were to replace - at Manchester Central in 1960.** Alan Bryant/*www.railphotoprints.co.uk.*

The English Electric 'Baby Deltic' was a spectacular failure with the whole class going through rebuilding within five years of construction. In July 1963 D5905 heads a row of stored Class 23s at Stratford awaiting return to Vulcan Foundry for rebuilding. Colin Whitfield/www.railphotoprints.co.uk.

Perhaps the most successful of the Type 2 diesels, particularly after new engines were installed, were the Brush-built Class 31s which came in at the top end of the classification's power spectrum. On May 6 1987 31302 approaches Melton Mowbray with 8E39, the 1.55pm Loughborough-March ballast. www.railphotoprints.co.uk.

These 58 locomotives were set to work on the branch lines of Devon and Cornwall but were underpowered compared to the Type 3 Hymeks and work for them began to dry up as lines were closed during the Beeching era. All had been taken out of service by 1971 and unfortunately none of the NBL locomotives from either batch made it into preservation.

There was also a rare 'turkey' from English Electric in the Type B category with their infamous 'Baby Deltics', which would have become Class 23 had they survived long enough. The idea of this design was to use a lightweight high-revving power unit to provide a compact locomotive with relatively high power which would be suitable for accelerated suburban duties. Unfortunately what resulted was a very complicated piece of kit which had a weight not much different from other offerings in the Type B category.

The nine-cylinder Delta engine produced 1,100hp but it was smoky, which meant that it got itself banned from the sub-surface Moorgate lines and in addition the heavier than anticipated weight meant the 'Baby Deltic' couldn't be used on many of the envisaged routes. Reliability was a big issue with the class only achieving about a quarter of the miles per casualty of other Type 2s and within the first couple of years there had been 44 engine changes amongst the 20 locomotives. No more were ordered after the pilot batch and they were all gone by 1971, except for one which stayed on in departmental service until 1975. Currently there is a project under way to build a replica using a heavily modified Class 37 bodyshell.

The most unusual offering in the Type B category came from Metropolitan-Vickers, with its Co-Bo design. The idea was to evaluate whether a Crossley low-revving two-stroke power unit gave any advantages over the more complicated four-stroke types. This design came in at 97tons and had to be given an additional axle to spread the weight which meant that it expended much of its power on moving itself around. In addition the two-stroke engines proved very smoky and vibration was a serious issue.

The class was allocated to the Midland and became famous for their use on the 'Condor'

overnight freight trains, for which they had to be used in pairs, but they also worked secondary passenger and freight with differing amounts of failure. As soon as possible the Midland Region despatched them off en-masse to the far-flung outpost of Barrow where they ended their days on local freight and passenger work and they were withdrawn as soon as was decently possible, all being out of capital service as early as 1968. The pilot batch of 20 was not added to, even in the heady days of mass dieselisation, which perhaps says a great deal about how unsuccessful this design was.

A false economy?

With hindsight it is surprising that British Railways spent so much time and money on the Type B diesel locomotives. All were underpowered when compared with modern 4-6-0 and 4-6-2 mixed traffic steam designs and it is difficult to understand exactly what work was envisaged for them. When put to work on suburban services many were found wanting and in places such as Scotland they had to be used in pairs in order to provide the required horsepower for working trains. Almost as soon as considerable numbers were in service BR was scrambling to find something more powerful, leading to the proliferation of classes such as the 37, which were to prove extremely capable as go anywhere do anything machines.

It is likely though that management thought there would always be a need for locomotives for secondary services, without realising that many of the secondary and branch services would themselves soon cease to exist. Inevitably that left a glut of Type Bs, explaining why so many went to the scrapyards after a relatively short life. Others, such as the 25s, 26s and 27s were extremely successful and went on to perform work which perhaps was never envisaged for them when they were built.

Whatever the reasoning behind the ordering of the various Type B, or Type 2 designs, we have been left with a rich legacy which has done much to add to the success of the railways over the last half century. ■

ROLLING STOCK
& operation

With the scenic aspects of Shortley Bridge and Felton Cement Works all but complete **MIKE WILD** describes the rolling stock that will operate on it and how the layout will work at exhibitions.

BR '4MT' 76109 crosses Shortley Bridge viaduct with a mixed goods.

BUILDING A MODEL RAILWAY is only half of the story and even when it reaches the stage of being a complete scenic display there is still the important consideration of which trains will run on it and how it will work.

Shortley Bridge and Felton Cement Works, like the majority of *Hornby Magazine's* layouts, will only be assembled and run when it attends exhibitions. It might surprise you to know that during the build period for this new layout it has only had the bare minimum of train operations to test the track and electrics. In fact at this point it has never had a full running session as such, partly due to the 12 week schedule to assemble it.

It has been designed to operate with Digital Command Control (DCC) following on from the standards established by the Operation Build It! terminus station. This was wired purely for DCC operation and features Train-Tech accessory decoders for the points and the same manufacturer's specially designed accessory decoders for the Dapol semaphore signals which protect the station. The control system at the centre of this is the Gaugemaster Prodigy – a reliable system from our experience which is simple to operate and learn.

The new baseboards for the extension all use the same equipment throughout with heavy duty speaker cable being used as the power bus

┌o┐2 Clayton Type 1 D8600 departs Felton Cement Works with a set of loaded Presflos.

to transmit DCC signals around the layout. However, when it comes to running the layout in exhibition conditions we will need more than one control point.

The plan is that one operator will be positioned at the station area with a controller connection located to give them maximum freedom of movement while a second operator will be positioned alongside the cement works. Between these two positions all train movements will be handled which should result in a good flow of traffic around the layout. However, being a single track branch line, we will have to work hard to maintain activity levels on the cement works side when the main line is otherwise occupied.

In order to provide these control points Shortley Bridge will share a pair of Gaugemaster Prodigy extension sockets with Twelve Trees Junction. This will materials being

stored out of use when they could otherwise be of service on a layout. These extension panels allow the Prodigy base station to be connected to any number of control points around a layout offering maximum flexibility in operation.

Fiddle yard design

One of the most important aspects of Shortley Bridge is still to be built – the fiddle yard. During construction we used the turntable storage yards from Ashland to support basic operations in our workshop. However, in scenarios such as the Warley Model Railway Exhibition, where Shortley Bridge will be making its debut in November, the limitations posed by these fiddle yards are too great.

In principle it is a reliable and useful space saving system, but in exhibition situations (and with a layout of this size) ideally we need to have greater flexibility and ease of operation. It should also make operations more fluid by maximising the amount of time trains are on view in the scenic section. Equally when necessary we really need Shortley Bridge to be suitable for one man operation so there is a plan to build a bespoke fiddle yard for the layout.

This will consist of three new baseboards mirroring those built for the corners and viaduct scene and as well as improving operation they will also assist greatly in the ease of transporting the layout to and from shows. »

The new fiddle yard will be a traditional ladder yard, but with a single track entrance and exit. However, with future layout proposals in mind this may be designed with a double track entrance to allow it be used with other layouts, improving its viability for construction. The most important aim of this though is that it enhances Shortley Bridge in the short term. Look out for more on this design in the *Hornby Magazine* Staff Projects pages.

Motive power

A healthy selection of motive power is available to Shortley Bridge and Felton Cement Works. It is nominally set in the North East, but we won't have a strict locomotive policy for the layout as there are a few items which are just too good not to have in the fleet. For example we have a Robinson 'C13' 4-4-2T from OO Works which is sound fitted plus a Bachmann Robinson 'J11' 0-6-0, also sound fitted, both of which wouldn't have run on the North Eastern Region being Great Central engines. Equally though we have a 'D11/2' 4-4-0 most commonly associated with Scotland. All three of these locomotives will make appearances on the layout.

Even taking these concessions into account though we do have a respectably accurate set of locomotives available. These include Hornby Thompson 'L1' 2-6-4Ts, Bachmann BR '3MT' 2-6-2Ts and '4MT' 2-6-4Ts, Bachmann 'J39' 0-6-0s, Bachmann BR '4MT' 2-6-0s and as well as larger locomotives such as the 'WD' 2-8-0 which will most likely be seen at the head of cement trains. Plus by the early part of 2015 we hope to be able to add a Peppercorn 'K1' 2-6-0 to the roster when Hornby releases its new model together with, one day, a DJ Models Raven 'Q6' 0-8-0 increasing the North Eastern theme of the

motive power fleet.

The diesel fleet available to Shortley Bridge is strong too with classes 17, 20, 24, 25, 27, 31 and 37 all part of the planned fleet, many of which have already been sound fitted for use on our previous exhibition layout Bolsover and Seven Lane Pit. You might also see a couple of off-region pilot scheme diesels too such as a Class 15 or 16 from time to time.

Happily Diesel Multiple Units (DMUs) are well represented in ready-to-run form and Shortley Bridge will be able to draw upon a Derby Lightweight two-car set, a two-car Class 101 or Class 105 and a choice of two-car and three-car Class 108s. There is also the possibility of four-car DMU operations with the new fiddle yard

offering another common train formation of DMUs working in multiple.

Choosing the exact locomotives for your layout, if you are basing it on a particular region, comes down to either knowledge or research. If you have read Tim Shackleton's feature on weathering the 'L1s' for Shortley Bridge you will have seen that not all locomotives of a particular class are suitable for the same area, but a little bit of creativity to make 67722 - a Great Eastern section engine - an ex-works engine on running-in turns from Darlington Works means we can have that extra touch of flexibility in what runs on the layout. And, of course, it is your layout at the end of the day and you can run what you like on it. »

3 Left: **Thompson 'L1' 2-6-4T 67777** crosses the road bridge on the approach to the cement works.

4 Below: **Brush Type 2 D5640** enters the yard at Felton Cement Works with a set of empty wagons. The Class 08 behind will take over, shunting wagons into the relevant sidings.

THE ROSTER		
CLASS	**MANUFACTURER**	**NOTES**
Thompson 'L1' 2-6-4T 67722	Hornby	Sound fitting planned
Thompson 'L1' 2-6-4T 67777	Hornby	Sound fitting planned
Robinson 'C13' 4-4-2T 67434	OO Works	Sound fitted, Zimo
Gresley 'J39' 0-6-0 64838	Bachmann	Sound fitted, ESU
Robinson 'J11' 0-6-0 64360	Bachmann	Sound fitted, ESU
Robinson 'D11/2' 4-4-0 62677	Bachmann	Sound fitted, ESU
BR '4MT' 2-6-0 76109	Bachmann	Sound fitting planned
BR '3MT' 2-6-2T 82029	Bachmann	Sound fitted, ESU
BR '4MT' 2-6-4T 80120	Bachmann	Sound fitted, ESU
BR 'WD' 2-8-0 90254	Bachmann	Sound fitted, ESU
Class 08 D3105	Hornby	Sound fitted, ESU
Class 17 D8600	Heljan	Sound fitting planned
Class 20 D8101	Bachmann	Sound fitting planned
Class 24 D5061	Bachmann	Sound fitted, ESU
Class 25 D5182	Bachmann	Sound fitted, ESU
Class 25 D7646	Bachmann	Sound fitted, Zimo
Class 27 D5353	Heljan	Sound fitted, Zimo
Class 31 D5640	Hornby	Sound fitted, ESU
Class 101 two-car DMU	Bachmann	Sound fitted, ESU
Class 108 two-car DMU	Bachmann	Sound fitted, ESU

Traffic patterns

There are three main traffic types which will run on Shortley Bridge. These consist of passenger, mixed goods and block cement workings. The inclusion of Felton Cement Works in this layout has created an additional reason for the railway to exist, whereas if we had built another station we might not have included these specific type of train formation.

Cement traffic is formed of two movements – incoming empty wagons which will run through Shortley Bridge station, sometimes being looped, and outgoing loaded wagons which will run back through Shortley Bridge. This will mean that a siding or two will be needed in the fiddle yard to accommodate this traffic type as well as modifications to a selected number of locomotives so that they are equipped for this traffic.

The modifications will be to the coupling arrangement. We are currently trying a number of different arrangements to do away with tension lock couplings on the front of locomotives including custom made brass

BR '4MT' 2-6-4T 80120 leads a passenger working past Felton Cement Works. In the yard a Clayton runs through the yard ready to couple up to a set of loaded Presflos.

loops which will allow full bufferbeam detail to be fitted to locomotives without losing the functionality of a tension lock coupling. This also takes away the need to change couplings on wagons too.

Uncoupling in the cement works will be handled manually using a plastic uncoupler made by Ron North of the High Wycombe and District Model Railway Society (HM31). This device is very handy and allows single handed uncoupling of wagons at any position in the yard. The same device will be used in the goods yard at Shortley Bridge.

The cement traffic flows will also result in plenty of shunting at the works where a resident shunter – usually a Class 03 or 08 – will be on hand to move wagons to relevant sidings for loading or stabling. A minimum of 16 cement wagons will be used for this traffic with one set of eight formed for each journey to or from the works.

Mixed goods traffic will mainly consist of pick up goods which will drop and collect wagons from Shortley Bridge goods yard. The factory »

6 Robinson 'C13' 4-4-2T 67434 clanks towards Shortley Bridge station as it slows for the stop with its rake of Thompson carriages.

at the station will also receive and despatch wagons as required allowing for a small amount of shunting in the yard. With Shortley Bridge only having a single platform face only one passenger train will operate on the layout at any time meaning that any passing movements in the station will see a freight train cross with a passenger working. Freights may also be held in the loop to be overtaken by a passenger working.

Passenger traffic on the branch will be limited to three carriage trains. This was originally limited by space in the turntable fiddle yards, but even with the planned new larger fiddle yard this train length will be retained as it suits the railway perfectly.

The train formations will be made up of Gresley and Thompson non-corridor stock as well as a set of three BR maroon Mk 1s and possibly a trio of Gresley corridor carriages depending upon what stock is required for exhibitions. Beyond this DMUs will be an additional component of the passenger service with a Class 101 and Class 108 already sound fitted with plans to add sound to a Cravens Class 105 unit for the layout too.

The future

Like every layout we build, the point where we finish the Yearbook is never the end of the project. Shortley Bridge and Felton Cement Works will be coming back into our workshop in

With the dramatic scenery of the valley below a Clayton Type 1 leads an empty rake of Presflos towards Felton Cement Works.

early November for finishing off including fitting fascia panels, making it suitable for transport and construction of the new fiddle yard.

Detailing will continue too and hopefully by the time of the Warley National Model Railway Exhibition on November 21/22 it will have taken a few more steps forward in both its appearance and in the way it runs. Plus we'll be finishing off more of the locomotive fleet including adding sound to the new pair of 'L1s'

and the Class 17 – fingers crossed!

The North Eastern theme for Shortley Bridge sets it out as something different to all our previous layouts for the Yearbook which have covered the Western (HMYB4), Southern (HMYB6) and Midland (HMYB5) regions. We've thoroughly enjoyed creating this layout and we hope that it is well received on the exhibition circuit as it will be on show several times in 2015 for *Hornby Magazine*. ∎

The peace is shattered at Shortley Bridge station as Sulzer Type 2 rumbles into the station with a through ballast working.

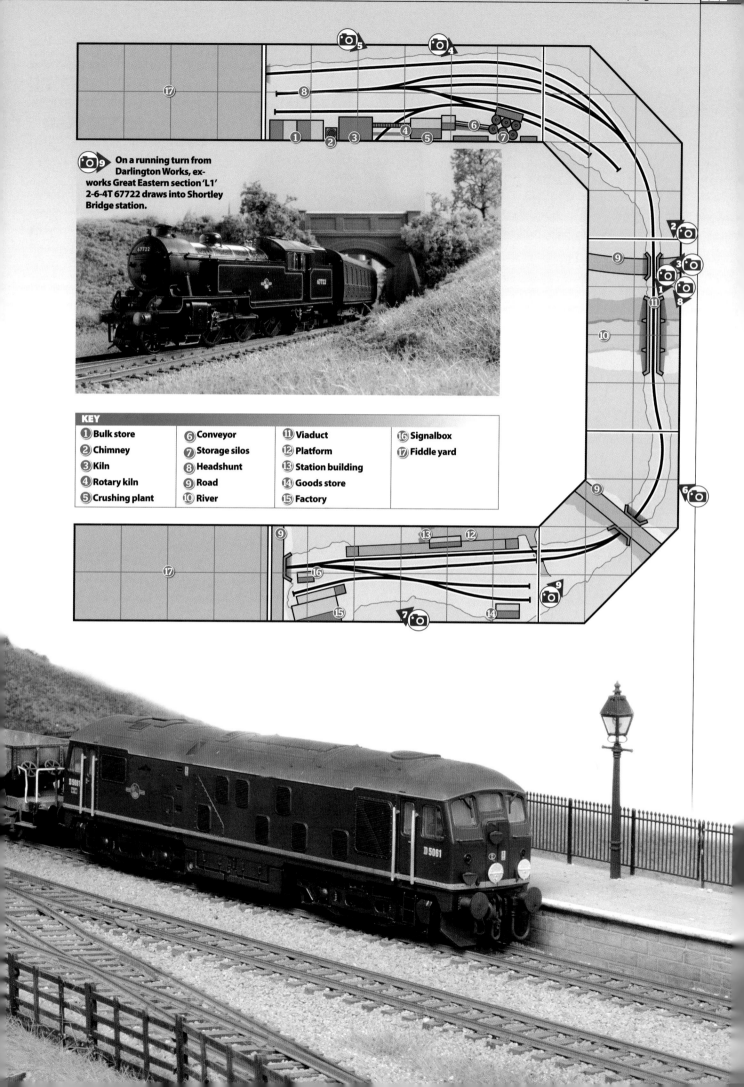

On a running turn from Darlington Works, ex-works Great Eastern section 'L1' 2-6-4T 67722 draws into Shortley Bridge station.

KEY

① Bulk store	⑥ Conveyor	⑪ Viaduct	⑯ Signalbox
② Chimney	⑦ Storage silos	⑫ Platform	⑰ Fiddle yard
③ Kiln	⑧ Headshunt	⑬ Station building	
④ Rotary kiln	⑨ Road	⑭ Goods store	
⑤ Crushing plant	⑩ River	⑮ Factory	

Forward to 2015

Last year saw some amazing models released – but there's plenty more to come over the next 12 months. **MIKE WILD** looks to the future and discovers more than 80 new locomotives across three scales are on the cards for 2015 and beyond.

THE PAST YEAR has been astonishing in terms of the quality of new models on sale but perhaps more notably for the rate of announcements of forthcoming releases. So much so that there are more than 80 new locomotives and multiple units which are due for release across 'OO', 'N' and 'O' scales.

2014 saw the release of 13 new locomotives in 'OO' plus six in 'N' gauge by the end of September, but by comparison 'OO' alone is set to receive another 39 new locomotives and multiple units over the next two years covering all manner of designs.

Announcements have come thick and fast and in a year when the release of new models has been comparatively slow we've certainly been treated to an impressive raft of new prospects. In this preview to the new announcements we have barely scratched the surface as we are only covering locomotives and multiple units. If we took new carriage and wagon plans into account the list would be much, much bigger.

'OO' gauge

As the most popular scale in British railway modelling 'OO' gauge has the greatest number of new projects on offer. What is most impressive about these is the sheer range of locomotive designs which are set for release, covering everything from 0-4-0 tank engines through express giants such as the GWR 'King' 4-6-0 and the GNR 'C1' 4-4-2.

In total there are 23 new steam locomotives promised for 'OO' gauge with only the London Midland Region losing out, though in fairness many of the principal types are the subject of very good models already. Here there are only two new models on the cards – the Stanier '5MT' 2-6-0 and the Webb 'Coal Tank' 0-6-2T – both from Bachmann, but it is the South West which »

Gresley 'D16/3' 4-4-0 62571 passes Meadow Lane as its departs Nottingham with the 2pm Derby-Lincoln on May 18 1957. The 'D16/3' is to be released in 'OO' gauge by Hornby. Gordon Hepburn/Rail Archive Stephenson.

Hornby's Crosti '9F' 2-10-0 broke cover in the summer with this first look at the new tooling.

DJ Models revealed its first engineering prototype for the new 'OO' gauge Hunslet 'Austerity' 0-6-0ST in September.

Locomotion Models and Bachmann are hard at work developing a GNR 'C1' 4-4-2 for 'OO' gauge. It will be released in GNR, LNER and BR liveries.

Rails of Sheffield is continuing to work closely with Bachmann to develop its models of LMS prototypes 10000 and 10001 in original condition.

TABLE 1 - 'OO' GAUGE NEW RELEASES FOR 2014-2015

Class	Region	Manufacturer	Expected
GWR '1361' 0-6-0ST	Western	Kernow MRC	2015
GWR '1361' 0-6-0ST	Western	Heljan	2015
GWR '1366' 0-6-0ST	Western	Heljan	2015
GWR 'Hall' 4-6-0	Western	Hornby	Late 2014
GWR '64XX' 0-6-0PT	Western	Bachmann	2015
GWR 'King' 4-6-0	Western	Hatton's	2015/2016
GWR 'King' 4-6-0	Western	Hornby	2015
LSWR 'O2' 0-4-4T	Southern	Kernow MRC	Late 2014
LSWR 'B4' 0-4-0T	Southern	Dapol	2015
LBSCR 'E4' 0-6-2T	Southern	Bachmann	2014
LBSCR 'I3' 4-4-2T	Southern	OO Works	2015
LBSCR 'H2' 4-4-2T	Southern	Bachmann	2015
SR 'USA' 0-6-0T	Southern	Bauer Media	2015
LNWR 'Coal Tank' 0-6-2T	Midland	Bachmann	2016
LMS '5MT' 2-6-0	Midland	Bachmann	2015
GER 'J15' 0-6-0	Eastern	Hornby	2015
GNR 'C1' 4-4-2	Eastern	NRM/Bachmann	2015
LNER 'Q6' 0-8-0	Eastern	DJ Models	2015/2016
LNER 'O2' 2-8-0	Eastern	Heljan	2015
LNER 'D16/3' 4-4-0	Eastern	Hornby	2014
LNER 'K1' 2-6-0	Eastern	Hornby	2014/2015
BR Crosti '9F' 2-10-0	Midland/Eastern	Hornby	2015
LNER 'J94' 0-6-0ST	Eastern	DJ Models	2015
Hudswell Clarke 0-6-0ST	Industrial	DJ Models	2015/2016
AEC GWR railcar	Western	Dapol	2015
Bulleid 10201-10203	Southern	Kernow MRC	TBC
LMS 10000/10001	Midland	Rails of Sheffield	2015
Class 05	Scottish	Heljan	2015
Class 21/29	Scottish	Dapol	2015
Class 24/1	Various	Bachmann	2015
Class 41 'Warship'	Western	Kernow MRC	TBC
Class 43	Western	Bachmann	2015
Class 59	Western	DJ Models	2015/2016
Class 71	Southern	DJ Models	2015
Class 73	Southern	Dapol	2015
Class 90	Various	Bachmann	2016
Class 143	Western	Realtrack Models	2015
Class 158	Various	Bachmann	2015
APT-E	Western	Rapido Trains	2015
Metropolitan Railway Bo-Bo	Underground	Heljan	2015
Park Royal railbus	Midland/Scottish	Heljan	2015
Wickham trolley	Various	Bachmann	TBA
L&B 2-6-2T ('OO9')	Southern	Heljan	TBA
Baldwin 4-6-0T ('OO9')	Industrial	Bachmann	2016

is gaining momentum at the moment and in particular the Great Western Railway (GWR).

In recent months attention has been focused on the GWR's locomotives by double announcements of two locomotive classes with both Kernow Model Rail Centre and Heljan working on separate projects for the GWR '1361' 0-6-0ST and Hatton's Model Railways and Hornby

both developing new models of the GWR's largest production express locomotive design, the 'King' 4-6-0. Duplication has occurred in the past with GWR models but as this Yearbook closed for press all four models were still going ahead.

The GWR is also set to receive new models of the '1366' 0-6-0PT, '64XX' 0-6-0PT and 'Hall' 4-6-0

with the latter due for release during October. The two 0-6-0PTs are substantially different with Heljan developing the outside cylinder short wheelbase '1366' and Bachmann the longer wheelbase 'auto fitted' '64XX'.

On the Southern five manufacturers are working on separate projects covering the LSWR 'O2' 0-4-4T and 'B4' 0-4-0T, LBSCR 'E4' 0-6-2T, 'I3' 4-4-2T and 'H2' 4-4-2 and the 'USA' 0-6-0T. All are in varying stages of production with the Adams 'O2' by Kernow Model Rail Centre set to lead the charge for Southern releases in late 2014 or early 2015.

Happily the Eastern Region is doing particularly well for new releases at the moment – an area which traditionally manufacturers didn't warm to. There are six new locomotives from the Eastern and North Eastern Regions in development ranging from the GNR 'C1' 4-4-2 from Locomotion Models to the Raven 'Q6' 0-8-0 from DJ Models and the Great Eastern 'J15' 0-6-0 and 'D16/3' 4-4-0 from Hornby. Least we forget Hornby is also

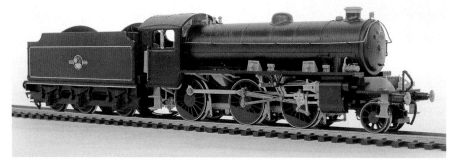

Hornby is firmly working on Eastern Region locomotives at present with three on the cards for release including the Peppercorn 'K1' 2-6-0. This new 'OO' model is expected around New Year, 2015.

Offering a first in British ready-to-run locomotives, DJ Models has launched a 'crowd sourcing' project to fund production of a BR Class 71 third-rail electric locomotive for 'OO' gauge with the support of Kernow Model Rail Centre. On July 9 1961 E5015 departs from Victoria with the 11am 'Golden Arrow' for Dover Marine. Brian Stephenson.

In late September Bachmann revealed the first images of its new NBL Class 43 'Warship' for 'OO' gauge.

TABLE 2 - 'N' GAUGE NEW RELEASES FOR 2014-2015

Class	Region	Manufacturer	Expected
GWR '64XX' 0-6-0PT	Western	Bachmann	TBC
GWR 'Castle' 4-6-0	Western	Bachmann	TBC
GWR 'Grange' 4-6-0	Western	Dapol	2015
GWR '63XX' 2-6-0	Western	DJ Models	2015
SR 'Merchant Navy' 4-6-2	Southern	Bachmann	TBC
SR 'West Country' 4-6-2	Southern	Dapol	2015
SR rebuilt 'West Country' 4-6-2	Southern	Dapol	2015
SR 'Schools' 4-4-0	Southern	Dapol	2015
SR 'N' 2-6-0	Southern	Bachmann	2015
LMS 'Duchess' 4-6-2	Midland	Bachmann	2014
LMS '4F' 0-6-0	Midland	Bachmann	2015
LNER 'J72' 0-6-0T	Eastern	Dapol	2015
LNER 'Q6' 0-8-0	Eastern	DJ Models	2015
LNER 'A2' 4-6-2	Eastern	Bachmann	2014
BR '4MT' 2-6-4T	Various	Bachmann	TBC
Hunslet 'J94' 0-6-0ST	Eastern	DJ Models	2015
Hudswell Clarke 0-6-0ST	Industrial	DJ Models	2015
Class 17	Eastern/Scottish	DJ Models	2015
Class 23	Eastern	DJ Models	2015
Class 31	Various	Bachmann	2015
Class 33	Southern	Dapol	2015
Class 37/4	Various	Bachmann	2014
Class 37/5	Various	Bachmann	2014
Class 47/7	Various	Bachmann	TBC
Class 50	Midland/Western	Dapol	TBC
Class 59	Western	DJ Models	2015/2016
Class 142	Midland/Eastern	Dapol	TBC
Class 390	Midland	Pendolino Project	TBC

TABLE 3 - 'O' GAUGE NEW RELEASES FOR 2014-2015

Class	Region	Manufacturer	Expected
LBSCR 'A1' 0-6-0T	Southern	Dapol	2015
LBSCR 'A1X' 0-6-0T	Southern	Dapol	2015
Hunslet 'J94' 0-6-0ST	Eastern	DJ Models	2015
Class 08	Various	Dapol	TBC
Class 23	Eastern	DJ Models	TBC
Class 25	Midland/Eastern	Heljan	TBC
Class 40	Midland/Eastern	Heljan	2014
Class 42	Western	Heljan	TBC
Class 45	Midland	Heljan	TBC
Class 60	Various	Heljan	2015
D0280 Falcon	Eastern/Western	Heljan	TBC
AC Cars railbus	Western	Heljan	2014

developing a ready-to-run model of the BR Crosti-boilered '9F' 2-10-0 which is being pitched as a top of the line RailRoad model.

Diesel traction is not being ignored despite huge inroads being made into what can be made in model form. Standout projects include Bachmann's new North British Locomotive Company Class 43 'Warship' which on first glance is set to be an outstanding model - and then there is Rapido Trains' first venture into British outline models with the Advanced Passenger Train – Experimental (APT-E) gas turbine prototype which is set for release in the first half of 2015. Electric locomotives are seeing increased interest too, with Dapol continuing work on its Class 73 electro-diesel, Bachmann announcing a Class 90 and DJ Models revealing a 'crowd sourcing' project to fund a model of the Southern Region's Class 71 electric.

Meanwhile Heljan continues to follow its own path with projects for the Park Royal four-wheel railbus, Hunslet Class 05 diesel shunter » and Metropolitan Railway Bo-Bo electric all in development. Kernow Model Rail Centre's NBL D600 'Warship' has also taken steps forward this year with a large scale model being sent out to its factory in China for assessment and detailed drawing work to continue.

A new diversion for 4mm scale ready-to-run is two announcements in narrow gauge, 'OO9'. In the first half of the year Heljan confirmed its previously announced plans for the Lynton and Barnstaple Railway 2-6-2T and at its catalogue launch in July Bachmann revealed its intention to develop a model of the Baldwin 4-6-0Ts introduced during the First World War for military railways.

'N' gauge

In the smaller scale Bachmann, Dapol and DJ Models are fighting it out for new projects with 28 new projects – 17 steam, 11 diesel – planned by the trio.

Like 'OO' gauge steam is still king in 'N' gauge with the Southern Region leading the charge with five locomotives in development, beating the Western by one. The Eastern Region sees three steam locomotives in development while, like in 'OO' gauge, the Midland lags behind with only two new models expected. However, looking back on recent releases the Midland has faired well in the past few years in 'N' with 2014 alone seeing the Fairburn 2-6-4T and 'Jinty' 0-6-0T released to join a collection which includes the 'Black Five', 'Jubilee' and 'Royal Scot' 4-6-0s amongst others.

A significant new development for 'N' gauge sees DJ Models carving itself a niche for industrial locomotives. It was already developing a new model of the Hunslet 0-6-0ST from the company's launch in 2013, but this year has seen the manufacturer announce it plans for a Hudswell Clarke 0-6-0ST too. It is also working on a Raven 'Q6' 0-8-0 for 'N'.

In the diesel stakes there is a wide range of projects in the offing ranging from the ill-fated Class 17 Clayton diesels through to the forerunner of the Class 66, the Class 59 – both from DJ Models. Add to this new models of the Class 31, 33 and 50 and 'N' gauge has a lot to offer.

'O' gauge

Of the three main scales for British models 'O' gauge has seen the least growth in terms of planned releases with the same total of 12 for 2013 following through to 2014. However, these aren't all the same locomotives with Heljan having delivered its Class 52 'Western' and announced a project for Brush prototype D0280 *Falcon* during the latter half of 2014. In fact Heljan is investigating a model of diesel prototype HS4000 *Kestrel* for 'O' gauge too, but this is not a confirmed project at present.

The next big thing to arrive in 'O' gauge will be the Class 40 from Heljan, but this is expected to

Dapol's first 'O' gauge locomotive, the Stroudley 'A1' 0-6-0T, is making good progress. This is the first engineering prototype of the 7mm scale 'Terrier'.

be followed soon after by Dapol's first ready-to-run locomotive for the scale – the long lived London Brighton & South Coast Railway (LBSCR) 'Terrier' 0-6-0T. This model has been through a major redesign since the change of staff at Dapol in 2013 and it is to be released in both original 'A1' and rebuilt 'A1X' formats and in a range of liveries.

DJ Models' involvement with 'O' gauge has remained stable with the manufacturer retaining its commitment to the Hunslet 'Austerity' 0-6-0ST and Class 23 'Baby Deltic' for the scale, but it announced no new locomotive for 'O' gauge in 2014.

Overview

Reviewing the overall statistics makes for interesting reading. Looking back over the past three years it is no surprise 'OO' gauge is the largest growth market for new models and certainly where the manufacturers have faith in placing their investment. This is encouraging as we know that the 'OO' gauge market is by far the biggest and most accessible.

The addition of duplicate steam locomotives in the 'OO' gauge section isn't the best news, but it does show the strength of the hobby. Given the enduring popularity of the GWR, we hope all the models will be successful. The variety of locomotives that are being produced is impressive too. It is also noteworthy that ready-to-run production is turning in two directions – on the one hand steam models are generally being based on older designs whereas diesel and electric announcements, on the whole, are naturally turning towards the latest generation of motive power.

The greater fidelity of 'N' gauge models we've seen in recent years seems to be making steam locomotives a much more attractive prospect to modellers, while its stronghold in diesel and electric traction seems secure too. Plus, with

ready-to-run 'OO9' due to come on stream from Bachmann and Heljan within the next 18 months there are now new choices of modelling subject within easy reach of all modellers.

Another clear sign is that despite the mass introduction of diesel models, steam is still king when it comes to ready-to-run production and it is also encouraging to see growth in the number of tank engines being produced. Similarly, DJ Models' decision to continue producing industrial steam locomotives with the Hunslet and Hudswell Clarke 0-6-0STs is to be applauded as this is a large gap in the current marketplace with regular calls from *Hornby Magazine* readers for a better off the shelf selection.

The availability of ready-to-run products continues to develop and with Hornby's recent return to form we look set to have a very busy autumn and winter as more models from these lists reach the shops. We can't wait! ∎

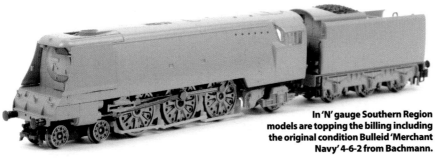

In 'N' gauge Southern Region models are topping the billing including the original condition Bulleid 'Merchant Navy' 4-6-2 from Bachmann.

At the end of the summer Rapido Trains began tooling work for its first British outline ready-to-run model – the APT-E gas turbine prototype for 'OO'.

THE HEADLINES

Planned 'OO' gauge new releases

	2012	2013	2014
Steam:	15	17	26
Diesel:	14	13	18
Total:	29	30	44

Planned 'N' gauge new releases

	2012	2013	2014
Steam:	10	15	17
Diesel:	14	15	11
Total:	23	30	28

Planned 'O' gauge new releases

	2012	2013	2014
Steam:	1	3	3
Diesel:	6	9	9
Total:	7	12	12
Overall total:	59	72	82

GWR 'King' 4-6-0 6003 *King George IV* **approaches Savernake Low Level with the up 'Mayflower' from Plymouth to London Paddington on June 13 1959. The GWR's largest 4-6-0 is currently the subject of two new projects for 'OO' gauge through Hatton's and Hornby.** Ken Cook/Rail Archive Stephenson.

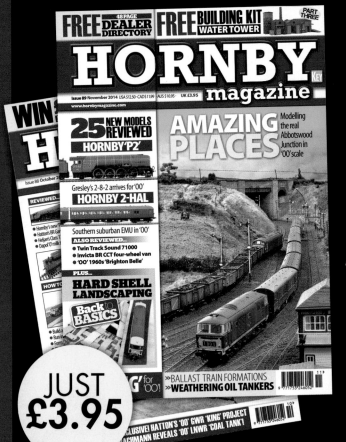
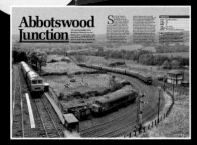